THE GOD CATCHERS
WORKBOOK

THE GOD CATCHERS WORKBOOK

EXPERIENCING THE MANIFEST PRESENCE OF GOD

TOMMY TENNEY

THOMAS NELSON PUBLISHERS®
Nashville

ISBN 0-7852-6623-2

Printed in the United States of America

01 02 03 04 05 VG 5 4 3 2

CONTENTS

INTRODUCTION

Many of the people whose lives were affected by *The God Catchers*—and *The God Chasers* before that—are eager to go deeper and farther in their pursuit of God. I know only a little, but I am willing to share whatever I have discovered in my journey of hot pursuit.

If you or the members of your Bible study class are included in this group of determined God Chasers, then it is for you that I prepared this workbook with the "Berean principle" in mind.

The writer of the book of Acts wrote something immediately after he described the apostle Paul's address to the Jews of Berea that is rare today. I'm sure the writer (presumably Luke the physician) was glad that they initially received his message, but he openly praised the Bereans because they didn't stop there!

Unlike many modern believers, the Jews of Berea were careful to check everything Paul said against the Scriptures to see if it was true:

The brethren immediately sent Paul and Silas away by night to Berea. When they arrived, they went into the synagogue of the Jews. These were more fair-minded than those in Thessalonica, in that they received the word with all readiness, and searched the Scriptures daily to *find out* whether these things were so. (Acts 17:10–11, emphasis added)

I want you to do the same thing the Bereans did. No one but God can see the whole picture. All of us are limited to seeing in part, and I am no exception to this truth. For that reason, I encourage you to study the Scriptures to assure yourself that the things I've said and written are true.

Each chapter of *The God Catchers Workbook* is designed to provoke thought and encourage personal application of the Bible truths contained in *The God Catchers* (unless otherwise indicated, the page numbers cited refer to that text). I've never been interested in pursuing—or asking others to pursue—mere busywork in the name of Bible study. Each exercise in these chapters was written with a very specific purpose in mind.

Sections titled "Erroneous Assumptions, Presumptions, and Misaligned Paradigms," for instance, are designed to expose and encourage careful examination of specific nonbiblical paradigms, practices, or thought patterns that are accepted in many modern churches, despite their extrabiblical origins.

Anytime you see the heading "What Do You Think?", expect to provide your opinion about the way your life, worship, service, and witness are affected by the clash between conflicting attitudes or mind-sets.

In the end, my hope and prayer are that you become a lifelong God Chaser and, by God's grace and through your own persistence, a God Catcher as well!

Remember that *The God Catchers Workbook* is a tool to help you draw closer to Him and grow deeper in your Christian faith. It is not a race, so your goal should not be to rush to the finish line first. Take your time, bathe the

Bible study process in prayer, rely on the Holy Spirit, and above all, seek the face of God. David the psalmist once told the wisest man in the world:

As for you, my son Solomon, know the God of your father, and serve Him with a loyal heart and with a willing mind; for the LORD searches all hearts and understands all the intent of the thoughts. If you seek Him, He will be found by you. (1 Chron. 28:9)

May God speed you in the chase, and bless you in the catching!

Tommy Tenney

DOES GOD PLAY HIDE-AND-SEEK?

THINGS I WISH I KNEW THE DAY I NEARLY CAUGHT HIM

God does not hide so that He cannot be found;
He is very careful to hide so that He can be found. (p. 12)

The first sentence in the first chapter of *The God Catchers* asks, "Have you ever wondered why it sometimes feels as if God is hiding from you?"[1] Why would I start a book with a question like this? The answer has everything to do with the subject of the book. It is a question every honest follower of Christ must ask and answer if he ever hopes to successfully "chase and catch" God.

Erroneous Assumptions, Presumptions, and Misaligned Paradigms

What assumptions or beliefs would make the terms *God Chaser* and *God Catcher* seem offensive to someone? Check any of the beliefs or religious paradigms that you believe may prevent people from chasing or catching God:

❑ God does *not* hide.

❑ God cannot be "caught" by anyone or anything.

❑ God really doesn't care about us as individuals, especially in the sense of having a personal relationship with us. After all, He is the almighty Creator. He doesn't have the time or desire to concern Himself with our petty desires and needs.

❑ We have nothing that God wants.

❑ Human beings are not worthy of God's attention; therefore, they don't get His attention.

❑ I'm already saved, so God lives in me and I don't have to chase Him. The Bible doesn't tell me to "do" anything other than believe and receive Jesus as Savior.

1. Have you wondered about any of these statements or beliefs? Where were you taught to believe these things? What do you think about them now?

2. I mentioned on page 2 of *The God Catchers* that God "launched me on a journey of His own choosing when He interrupted my self-defined successful career as a full-time evangelist." Can you describe what is meant by "a journey of His own choosing"? If you feel God has also launched you on a journey of His own choosing, try to describe it in two sentences or less.

What Do You Think?

God shocked me with a revelation contained in one simple comment (from p. 2, *The God Catchers*): *"You know, Tommy, your favorite services and My favorite services are not the same. You leave your services full and satisfied, but when you leave, I'm still hungry."*

1. What do you think God meant when He said He left my favorite services "hungry"? What do we have to offer that God could possibly desire or consume? What on earth does He look and search for? (Read John 4:23–24 and jot down your answer.)

2. What do you think makes a church service full and satisfying?

3. What do you think God thinks about your church service? Why?

4. What do you think about the statement "God will leave our meetings full and satisfied only when we begin to leave them feeling hungrier for Him than when we first came"? How can you leave a great time of worship in His presence feeling "hungrier" for Him than when you first came?

5. I mention on page 2 that the Lord began to teach me about the importance of being a God Chaser during a nine-month period of what I call "divine discontent." What do you think? What is "divine discontent," and is there a biblical basis for it? (Hint: Read about Jeremiah's "fire in his bones" in Jer. 20:9–11, and consider the words of the psalmist in Ps. 42 before answering this question.)

Special Resource Tip: Read Chapter 1, "The Day I Almost Caught Him," in *The God Chasers* for a better understanding of "divine discontent," and its role in revival and the pursuit of God's presence.[2]

FILLING THE VOID

Find this statement on page 3 of *The God Catchers* and fill in the "void" places. How many, if any, of these words apply to your life and your heart's desire?

Now I am no longer content just to "_____" Him. I want to "_____" Him, to collect a _____ of _____ _____ with Him. Sometimes I grow _____ with the daily chase, but I must _____ if I want to _____.

More Erroneous Assumptions, Presumptions, and Misaligned Paradigms

Read the statements reprinted here from page 3 of *The God Catchers*, where I describe how God taught me through my youngest daughter how and why He "hides" from us. Then glance back at the assumptions or beliefs listed earlier in this study guide chapter:

I tracked her every step as she looked for me in all the strange places that seem so logical from a toddler's point of view . . .

With growing anticipation I listened to my little pursuer's every move because I had a plan in mind.

List all of the assumptions or beliefs mentioned previously that are challenged by these statements:

Now read this passage from the book of Jeremiah:

"I know the plans I have for you," declares the LORD, "plans to prosper you and not to harm you, plans to give you hope and a future. Then you will call upon me and come and pray to me, and I will listen to you. You will seek me and find me when you seek me with all your heart. I will be found by you," declares the LORD. (Jer. 29:11–14 NIV, emphasis added)

Look at your list of erroneous assumptions, presumptions, and misaligned paradigms; and think about how many of them God challenges just in this one passage from His Word.

What Do You Think?

Please read this brief excerpt from page 4 of *The God Catchers:*

If it was clear that my petite pursuer was having trouble finding me, then I would be careful to leave something showing to help her along. If I was behind the closet door, then I'd make sure part of my foot was showing. If I took refuge behind the couch, then I'd make sure that just enough of my backside showed to help her find me.

Why be so careful? It is simple: the point of our elaborate game of hidey-face wasn't the hiding; *it was the finding!* I wasn't hiding from my little girl so that she couldn't find me; I was careful to hide so that she *could* find me.

Then I remembered that God did the same thing with Moses.

Read Exodus 33:22–23, and describe how God "did the same thing" with Moses that parents often do with their children when they grow discouraged while playing hide-and-seek.

TAKE IT PERSONALLY!

On page 5 of *The God Catchers,* we confront another common assumption about the supposed disinterest of God in our affairs. Look up 1 Peter 5:7, and read this brief excerpt from Chapter 1:

> Often, when we wander off in the wrong direction in our pursuit of Him, God calls out to us to help us along. When my youngest daughter and I played hidey-face, I loved to hear the lyrical sounds of her "little girl giggle" just bubbling with excitement. I loved it so much that if she wandered off in the wrong direction and stopped giggling in her search, then I would call out and say, "Over here . . . closer . . ."
>
> Then I would listen to her stop and *be still* while she tried to locate the source of Daddy's voice. *I am convinced that God does the same thing.*

How about you? Are you convinced? Take this truth about God's revealed nature and embrace it. Allow it to transform and change the way you pursue His face and relate to Him.

Dig Deeper

(MINING FOR GOLD IN THE FINE PRINT OF THE ENDNOTES)

On page 6 of *The God Catchers,* I said, "At least eleven times in the Psalms, David said in effect, 'You are a God who hides Himself . . .'" Then I put some vital information in the endnotes.

Just as in the natural realm, some of the most precious and valuable things can be found only by digging into the deeper places beyond the easy reach of casual seekers, so are some of the most valuable truths hidden in the endnotes and footnotes of books and articles.

The apostle Paul praised one group of believers because they weren't content to simply take his word about eternal things—they went straight to the Word of God to find the truth for themselves. That is exactly where I hope you go when you look up the endnotes in *The God Catchers*.

You have already read what God said about "hiding and finding" through Jeremiah the prophet. Now study the Psalms and confirm for yourself the fact that God sometimes hides from us. Look up these references reproduced from the endnotes of *The God Catchers*: Psalms 10:1; 13:1; 27:9; 44:24; 55:1; 69:17; 88:14; 89:46; 102:2; 104:29; 143:7.

REMEMBER THIS

She was immersed in the liquid joy of discovery and delighted by the unexpected excitement and serendipitous moment of encounter, *"It's him!"* Then we enjoyed about thirty seconds of sheer pleasure as we went through our private process of rediscovery and delight . . .

When I finally set her down, she wanted to kiss me again.

At that point, I would usually turn away. "Why?" you may ask. "Didn't you want to be kissed?" Of course, I did, but I knew that if I turned away, it would make my little girl pursue me even harder and she would give me even more kisses. It was a very well-organized plot. *I didn't run away*—I turned away. God doesn't leave either—He lingers. His greatest joy is to extend and expand the moments of encounter. Sunday morning kisses are not enough! (pp.7–8)

FILLING THE VOID

1. After reading through this brief passage from pages 7–8 of *The God Catchers*, do you remember what God seems to "extend and expand"? _____ of _____

2. When we feel as if God has "run away" from us, it may be that He has simply _____ away. He doesn't _____ either—He _____. Perhaps He is simply trying to extend and expand the _____ of _____ with *you* He enjoys so much.

What Do You Think?

At this point, you have probably read all the way through *The God Catchers*. Now I want you to read through a brief passage from page 8 of *The God Catchers,* in which I discuss the way my youngest daughter "captured" my heart. Then I want to ask your opinion about something.

She couldn't capture me physically, but she easily captured me emotionally. She couldn't move her legs fast enough to apprehend me, but her words easily captured my heart.

Some people take offense at my use of the term *God Chaser,* saying, "You don't have to chase God." I understand but I don't agree. You may call it whatever you want; it doesn't bother me. My youngest daughter didn't have to chase me to get me to be her daddy, but if she wanted more than just to live in the same house, if she wanted attention and affection, then she knew which "buttons" to push. You may be content just to be in God's house, but I want to be in His lap!

Now for your opinion on this statement, please check the statements you feel are true:

❑ "God Chasing" isn't the way we "work" our way into heaven or God's kingdom. (That comes only when we confess our sins and turn away from them, and confess that Jesus Christ is the Son of God and receive Him as our Savior and Lord.)

❑ A God Chaser is someone who already belongs to God's family, but wants to be close to Him, not just an acquaintance, a house guest, or a distant relative.

❑ A God Chaser—and especially a God Catcher—isn't ashamed to display hunger, desire, and ambition to be close to the heart of God. It becomes the most treasured goal on earth.

❑ We chase God not because we "have to," but because we "get to"!

What About This?

Isn't it true that no one can really "catch" God?

FILLING THE VOID

This quote from page 8 of *The God Catchers* answers this question. Please fill in the voids as you find them:

I __ _____ that _____ of us can ever really catch Him. That much is _____. His ways are as far removed from ___ _____ as the east is from the west. None of us can _____ ___ through physical effort, mental gymnastics, or passionless spiritual exertion. "_____" can't catch Him, but an appeal to mercy and grace . . . !

The "catching" will come if you can ever get to that point of _____ _____ where you just say, "Oh, Daddy!" All of a sudden, you _____ and enrapture ___ _____ __ the God you can't ____ _____ any other way. The One you are _____ will suddenly become the One who _____ ___!

TAKE IT
PERSONALLY!

Worship turns the tables on the chase. It takes you to the point where you don't have to pursue Him because He begins to pursue you. If you are a worshiper, *God will track you down* . . .

Worship and spiritual hunger make you so attractive to God that your circumstances cease to matter anymore. He will move heaven and earth to find a worshiper. When you begin to worship with all your being and desire, your heart turns Him toward you. You capture His attention and attract His affection.

This quote from page 9 of *The God Catchers* contains one of the most important points in this book, and one of the most treasured things God has revealed to me through the Scriptures and in my personal experience. Note the **bold** sentences; I urge you to take them personally.

If you practice a lifestyle of praise and worship to God, then He will make it His practice to pursue you. If you question this statement, then I challenge you to carefully study the Psalms. You will find that David the worshiper communed with God throughout his life.

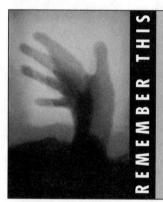

REMEMBER THIS

The joy of finding and being found was the purpose of the game. The hiding was just something I had to do to create the moment that I wanted. (p. 10)

If you understand this statement about why I hid from my daughters during games of hide-and-seek, then you will clearly understand what God showed me about why He hides from us from time to time.

What Do You Think?

On page 11 of *The God Catchers*, I describe the way my fatherly delight in my children motivated me to go to great lengths just to spend some special time with them:

I thought nothing of waking up at four o'clock in the morning after ministering in a long evening service and enduring six to eight hours in airports and on the plane just so I could experience thirty seconds of my daughter's joy in the driveway . . . God will take a trip in time just to spend a brief moment with humanity. He thinks it's worth it to be with you!

God loves it when you discover Him, but how can you discover Him if He doesn't sometimes hide?

1. What does it mean when I say that God will "take a trip in time" just to see us?[3]

2. Do you think I am exaggerating when I say that God is interested in spending time just with you (as if He actually knew your name)?[4] Why do you believe that, and how could I be correct in my assertion?

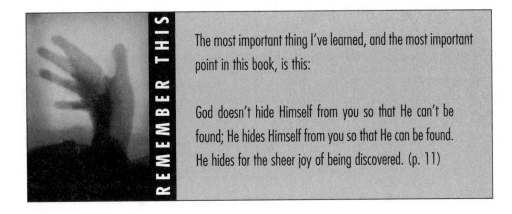

REMEMBER THIS

The most important thing I've learned, and the most important point in this book, is this:

God doesn't hide Himself from you so that He can't be found; He hides Himself from you so that He can be found. He hides for the sheer joy of being discovered. (p. 11)

What Do You Think?

The message in *The God Catchers* often challenges our ideas about "church as usual." Some people get upset because the things revealed in this book seem to bring into question virtually everything they've done in the name of "church" over the past few years. What do you think?

> We give Him a perfunctory kiss on Sunday morning and hurry to return to our religious toys and pretend encounters. All the while He is saying, "I've been missing you; I'd love to have some more loving kisses and hugs from you."
>
> God loves it when we want to linger in His presence, but those times are rare in most modern churches. We've become more time sensitive than Spirit sensitive. Whatever happened to "waiting on God"? (p. 12)

1. Does anything in these passages challenge "church" as you've known it in the past? If so, then describe the challenge.

2. Can you give some examples of what could be called "our religious toys and pretend encounters"?

3. In what ways are we more "time sensitive" than "Spirit sensitive"?

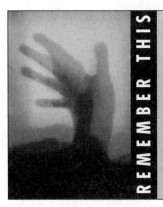

This book has one simple and straightforward focus: *how you can capture God's heart* . . . if you pursue His heart in passionate hunger, your words of desperation have the power to capture and "corner" His heart. In that moment, the Pursued becomes the Pursuer and the God Chaser becomes the God Catcher. (p. 12)

TAKE IT PERSONALLY!

Our problem in the church is that if we are not careful, the arrogance of our spiritual adolescence robs us of our childlike passion for His presence. More than anything else, we must learn that *God does not hide so that He* cannot *be found; He is very careful to hide so that He can be found.* (p. 12)

Arrogance and presumption have disqualified and dismissed us from God's presence since the first sin in the Garden of Eden. God sent His Son to take care of our sin problem, but He gave us this solution to the chronic attitude problem I call "the arrogance of our spiritual adolescence": "If My people who are called by My name will humble themselves and pray and seek My face and turn from their wicked ways, then I will hear from heaven and will forgive their sin and heal their land."[5]

The best way to begin the chase the right way is to begin the pursuit with humility, prayer, and hunger for Him.

NOTES

NOTES

2

BURNING LIPS AND HOT HEARTS

SOMEBODY CAUGHT HIM: THE TRUE STORY OF A GOD CATCHER

Break our hearts, Lord God. Set us on fire with incredible hunger
until nothing else and nothing less than Your presence will satisfy. (p. 30)

The first line of this chapter of *The God Catchers* includes another phrase that contains much more meaning than is implied by its brevity. It appears in the following paragraph with an endnote reference. This is where the "gold" for this phrase can be found.

Dig Deeper
(MINING FOR GOLD IN THE FINE PRINT OF THE ENDNOTES)

Are you part of the "restless remnant" that is incurably desperate for an encounter with God? The symptoms are unmistakable. Your compulsive addiction for God makes you sick of church games, man's manipulation, and passionless worship services consisting of religious stage gymnastics and emotional hype designed to excite and stroke the flesh. (p. 14)

FILLING THE VOID

The only way to really understand what is meant by "restless remnant" is to dig deeper and boldly go where few have gone before—into the endnotes of *The God Catchers* (pp. 193–94). Find the endnote and fill in the void as appropriate:

The "restless remnant" is my term for people ____ _____ _____ from their relationship with God than mere "_____ _____" or entrance to heaven someday when the Lord returns. They know there is more to following Christ than the _____ _____ of _____ . . . The restless remnant is comprised of "the ____, the _____, and the _____" who refuse to bow their knees to false gods, false messiahs, false shepherds, or trivial religious pursuits because they want only to ____ ____ _____ and dwell in ____ _____. The big problem with this remnant is that its members aren't easily cataloged, cross-referenced, or "boxed." Their only common characteristic (and the only prerequisite for membership) is their defining _____ for the _____ of the living God.

What Do You Think?

It should be obvious that no one can really "catch" God, but you can capture His heart. Once you do that, God allows you to pull Him into your dimension. (p. 14)

What do you think about this statement? One of the first things you should do to test any statement about God is to ask, "Are there any clear biblical precedents or examples of this in God's Word?" Now it is time to apply this test to the statement from page 14. Can you think of any incidents in the Old and New Testaments illustrating my claim? (Hint: See 1 Sam. 1:9–20 and Mark 10:46–52.)

Remember Where You've Been, But Always Dare to Dream

As you read this brief passage from page 15 of *The God Catchers*, think about your life and the times the voices of your children or family members suddenly transported you into their realm:

> How did that little girl physically pull my two-hundred-and-none-of-your-business pounds up from my place of thoughtful repose and transport me into her world as fast as my legs could carry me? Was it the strength of her little arms and delicate hands that did it? No, that is a physical and mathematical impossibility. She did it with her voice. There was an urgency to her cry.

Describe one or two of these incidents in your memory, and think about how they might apply to your own desire to "pull God into your dimension."

TAKE IT
PERSONALLY!

As you reread this passage from page 15, take the time to "take it personally."

Apparently the Old Testament prophet stumbled across God in the temple "before He had hidden Himself properly":

> In the year that King Uzziah died, I saw the Lord sitting on a throne, high and lifted up, and the train of His robe filled the temple.[1]

How many times did this prophet walk into the temple before that unforgettable day when he "caught" God? Isaiah wasn't the oldest or the most seasoned prophet alive in Judah that day, but he was the only one who saw the Lord "high and lifted up."

How many times have you walked into church services, only to leave unchanged, unchallenged, and uninspired to take up your cross more faithfully? We shouldn't always point our fingers and say, "It's the preacher's fault," or blame the worship leader for such a poor song selection. Nor should we think it takes more education, better training, or more experience. (You might discover it takes more hunger and desperation for Him.)

Erroneous Assumptions, Presumptions, and Misaligned Paradigms

None of us have room for two kings in our lives. It was only after King Uzziah finally died that the "other King" could rise up and say to Isaiah, "Now I'll let you see Me. You thought the glory of the former king was incredible; let Me show you My glory." (p. 16)

One of the best-known religious phrases in church circles warns, "Don't get so heavenly minded that you are no earthly good." It seems to me that the opposite danger is far more common and even more deadly. Perhaps we should start warning our children, "Don't get so earthly minded that you are no heavenly good." List what you feel are the top five "kings" competing with God for our affections in this life:

1.

2.

3.

4.

5.

REMEMBER THIS

After he caught sight of God taking His seat, Isaiah didn't see things the same way. He didn't say things the same way, and he didn't prophesy the same way.

What happened? Isaiah spent thirty seconds in the presence of the King, high and lifted up, and it utterly redirected, reformed, and transformed his life and ministry. (p. 16)

What Do You Think?

Sometimes my children come into my home because they have the "keys" to the door; they understand how to make an entrance as members of the family. Then there are times when their cries pull me from my world into their world. In that respect, they capture me by capturing my attention. Worship captures the attention of God, but it "pulls Him into our world" *when the circumstances are just right.* (p. 17)

What do you think some of those "circumstances" might be that can "pull Him into our world"?

What do you think are the "keys" to God's door? Can you think of any Scriptures that tell us "how to make an entrance as members of God's family"? (Hint: See Ps. 100:3–4; Heb. 10:19–22; James 4:5–10.)

More Erroneous Assumptions, Presumptions, and Misaligned Paradigms

In the following passage from page 18, I deal with a true assumption that is typically carried too far in practice. We wrongly use a general assumption about God to dismiss any possibility of His working or acting another way under specific circumstances. Can you perceive the problem as you reread this passage?

We must understand that God is always "there" in the sense that He is omniscient, and we know from His Word and from the historical record of human encounters with Him that He tends to move and act in somewhat predictable patterns. However, you can't perceive or "see" Him until you create the proper climate and the right atmosphere. Suddenly God seems to appear from nowhere, but in reality He is always there. The principles and laws governing His presence are constant. The problem isn't that God is "missing"; the problem is that you must get hot enough. Create the atmosphere!

The assumption is that God is _____, or present everywhere all the time. The assumption is true, but the idea that God cannot appear in any other way is *not true*. Consider these examples of God's "concentrated presence" or glory appearing on the earth:

1. Moses saw "the hinder parts of God" from the safety of a rock crevice (not to mention the residual glory of God glowing on his face; Ex. 33:18–23; 34:30–35).

2. What drove the priests out of Solomon's temple the day it was dedicated to God in the midst of worship and sacrifice? Was it His omnipresence or His shekinah glory revealed in the cloud? (See 1 Kings 8:10–12.)

3. What characteristic of the angel who rolled back the stone from the Lord's tomb caused battle-hardened Roman soldiers to drop to the ground as if they were dead? Was it the omnipresence of God? Was it the brightness of the light around them? Or was it the glory of God manifested through the angel? (See Matt. 27:62–28:4.)

4. What knocked Saul the persecutor to the ground and transformed him into Paul the martyr? (See Acts 9:3–6.) Why didn't everyone in the party fall to the ground and hear God's voice?

TAKE IT
PERSONALLY!

This truth drawn from the life of Isaiah the prophet on page 19 is so important that we have an obligation to "take it personally":

God cannot be King in your life until all other kings are gone. If you've been depending on the king of the fleshly realm, then the patterns of God's presence are never going to appear.

What Do You Think?

Where David offered brokenness and totally dependent love to God and was invited into God's inner chambers of intimacy, Uzziah assumed he was worthy and barged into God's chambers with an offering immersed in the fragrance of pride, arrogance, and presumption . . .

Perhaps the church suffers from the Uzziah Syndrome today. We insist on approaching God our way, and we say that everything is fine. Our way will be the acceptable way because we are sure we know what God likes. We think we can continue to "feed Him" like a trained pet on a chain with our crafted sermons, serial liturgies, and orchestrated prostrations in religious pride and arrogance. (p. 20)

What do you think? Does this sound familiar?

1. Think of the most recent church service in which you participated. Did the assembled saints approach God in "brokenness and totally dependent love"?

2. Did the church body approach Him under the assumption they were "worthy," offering Him praise and worship tainted by the odor of pride, arrogance, and presumption? (It is true that the blood of Jesus made us worthy, but the Lord did not shed His blood to give us a license to offend the heavenly Father with human pride, presumption, and disrespect!)

3. If your local church body is like most, its worship services are marked by a mixture of approaches. Humility and hunger mark some portions of the service, and the presumption of programmed religion dominates other portions of the service. Write down your observations.

TAKE IT PERSONALLY!

God has prescribed a cure for the problem of presumption, or what I call the Uzziah Syndrome, in this passage from page 21. As with many "cures" for life-threatening conditions, this treatment can be painful, and its effectiveness hinges on the willingness of the "patient" to see it through to the end. Are you willing to take it personally?

Has God turned away from us because of our empty religious forms? Has our presumption polluted our offerings and disqualified us from residence in His presence?

The only cure for the Uzziah Syndrome is an Isaiah experience with God that you will never get over. Most of us never make it to that point because we get angry when we are confronted with the truth. We get angry instead of yielding to sorrowful repentance, and we insist on swinging our sacred religious censers filled with unauthorized and unacceptable offerings. What we need are burning lips and a hot heart. One coal from His altar will cure our arrogance . . .

If you insist on retaining the rulership over your life, God will just evacuate and wait until something dies and dependency is re-created.

Notable Quotables to Ponder and Apply

Some people have a God-given knack for saying things in memorable ways. My father, T. F. Tenney, is one of those people. The Lord also blesses me from time to time with a phrase that seems to pack a lot of spiritual punch. As far as I'm concerned, all the honor goes to Him. He could have used a donkey, but He chose to give these "notable quotables" to me this time. Take a moment to ponder them in the light of God's Word, and then apply the truth you find to your life:

If you ever have an encounter with the manifest presence of God, it will ruin church for you. From then on, you put up with church. What you really want is, *"Come on, God."* (p. 24)

Circle true or false for each statement:

1. T / F The "church" referred to in this statement is the biblical bride of Christ first modeled in the first century and described in the New Testament.
2. T / F The "church" described here is really the man-centered, man-made, and man-empowered entity that has evolved from the "real thing" modeled in the New Testament, but often lacks any real proof of God's manifest presence.

3. T / F "Church" without passion for His presence is often empty religion. Church with passion for Him is a place where God and man meet together in supernatural union; where God comes first, and everything and everyone else follows His lead.

Your heavenly Father wants you to rediscover the joy of innocence and excitement at His presence. When we grow up to the arrogance of adolescence, we can't capture His heart because we think, *Oh, it's just You.* (p. 24)

Circle true or false for each statement:

1. T / F Adolescent arrogance says to God, "Been there, done that, Lord. Amuse me."
2. T / F Childlike faith says to God, "Oh, it's *You, Daddy!* I've missed You so much. Do it *again, Daddy. I want You* more than anything."

When passionate pleas replace dry discourses, "church" can become the celebration of His presence it was always meant to be. He was always there waiting, but the conditions were not correct. (pp. 24–25)

Circle true or false for each statement:

1. T / F Even exciting man-centered messages filled with scriptural quotations and skilled exegesis are dry when they lack hunger and thirst for the reality of God's manifest presence.
2. T / F Dry discourses are better suited for funeral services honoring departed loved ones than for celebrations honoring fresh reunions and discoveries.

When brokenness appears in our lives, openness appears in the heavens. (p. 25)

Circle true or false for each statement:

1. T / F   The opposite meaning of this might be: "When man's wholeness rules our lives, the heavens appear closed."
2. T / F   Brokenness seems to mark the opening of a doorway between divinity and humanity.

REMEMBER THIS

God will take advantage of your desperate feelings to create a dependency on Him. Thirty seconds in the manifest presence of God can change everything. It can change a nation, it can change your destiny, and it can rearrange your future. You'll never be the same. (p. 25)

TAKE IT
PERSONALLY!

If you are singing only because a song leader is singing, then you've stopped at the veil. But if suddenly you step out of this dimension and step into that one, you are not just worshiping because someone is leading; you begin worshiping because *He* is there . . .

If in infantile immaturity, you ever throw back the door and suddenly see Him, exclaiming, "There He is—Daddy!" then all you will ever want to do the rest of your life is to discover His presence. That is it. You will just want to be with Him. Never underestimate the potential of one service. (pp. 26–27)

More Erroneous Assumptions, Presumptions, and Misaligned Paradigms

This passage from pages 27–28 touches on a number of assumptions, presumptions, and misaligned paradigms that can become obstacles and stumbling blocks in our pursuit of God:

> Does God hide? Yes. That's the easy answer. But He doesn't hide so that He can't be found. He's very, very careful to hide so that He can be found. In His infiniteness, He could hide where you could never find Him, but He hides in the folds of time so that while you're singing a little song, praying a prayer, you discover Him. He didn't hide far away; He hid close. You can find Him in worship. Your passion is how you discover Him. Passion—not perfection—pulls God from His dimension into yours . . .

How do you get the conditions right to find Him?

1. You can pursue Him like a toddler. If you find His feet, you find His face.
2. At other times, desperation pulls Him from His dimension into yours. *He finds you!*

1. God hides . . .

❑ only because of our sin and hard-heartedness.

❑ so that we can't find Him.

❑ not so that He can't be found; He's very careful to hide so that He *can* be found.

2. To find Him, we *must* . . .

❏ attend a Tommy Tenney meeting (You'd better *not* choose this one).

❏ pursue Him as knowledgeable, logical adults and experienced churchgoers using proven techniques we learned through religious training.

❏ become like little children and humbly worship Him with passion and hunger "in spirit and in truth."

3. God's manifest presence is "pulled" into our dimension by . . .

❏ our magnificent worship services marked by the height of human perfection in composition, performance, and presentation.

❏ stunning sermons exhibiting exalted intelligence, remarkable self-controlled delivery, and the finest exegesis man can provide.

❏ mind-boggling edifices of worship featuring soaring spires, sparkling stained glass windows, state-of-the-art sound systems, thundering pipe organs, and specially designed full-comfort pews, carpet, and interior design.

❏ high-powered, high-speed, high-volume charismatic worship services guaranteed to simultaneously raise our blood pressure and burn off excess cholesterol.

❏ our passion and our desperation for Him.

TAKE IT
PERSONALLY!

These brief passages from page 28 summarize some of the most important things we've studied together in this chapter. Once again, you need to review the truth they contain and take it personally:

We have allowed the structure of man to impede the passion of a child . . .

As long as you are pretending everything is okay, He will allow you to go through it on your own. What He really wants to create is an air of dependency on Him. Quit trying to display your independence; start displaying your dependence and see what happens.

REMEMBER THIS

It is time to allow the king of all other pursuits to die. Let the pursuit of His presence become your single magnificent obsession. (p. 30)

NOTES

3

I Don't Know Whether to Laugh or Cry

CAUGHT IN THE MIDDLE OF WHAT IS AND WHAT CAN BE

If you find yourself feeling both grateful for His momentary visitation and desperately hungry for more, then I must say that you have no idea how close you are to an encounter with Him that will change your life. (p. 42)

Most of us are truly caught in the middle of what is and what can be. As difficult as this place may seem, we could be caught in an even worse place—we could be trapped and hopeless in the realm of what once was.

Much of the church seems to be bogged down in the mire of past visitations, second- and third-hand experiences with God, and the shadow of memorials to accomplishments completed in the distant past. This backward view stands in sharp contrast to the stated purposes of the unchanging God of eternity, the "God of the now" we serve.

Just as each individual must repent and receive Christ as Lord and Savior, so must each generation and local body of believers seek God's face, pursue fresh visitation today, and advance God's kingdom by faith.

As you continue your study, allow the questions, principles, and biblical truths highlighted from this chapter of *The God Catchers* to challenge your thinking and sharpen your hunger for more of God.

What Do You Think?

Sometimes I think that satisfaction may be the greatest enemy of the purposes of God in the church and in the world. Far too many God Chasers stop the chase to celebrate their best pace in the last race. We forget to resume the pursuit when we stop to build monuments to a momentary visitation of God's presence.

When we turn our focus from His face to the *memory* of His appearance yesterday, we may find that He has moved on to greater exploits outside our limited vision and perception of divine purpose. Jesus commanded us to take up our cross and follow Him *daily*—not as it fits in our schedule.[1] (p. 32)

1. What do you think about the danger of satisfaction? Have you experienced this in your life or observed it in others' lives?

2. What do you think causes us to "turn our focus from His face to the *memory* of His appearance yesterday"?

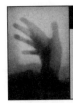

REMEMBER THIS

It is hunger that keeps us in the pursuit. (p. 32)

Erroneous Assumptions, Presumptions, and Misaligned Paradigms

So-called organized religion isn't necessarily evil or wrong. Doesn't God's Word require us to do all things "decently and in order"?[2] The purpose of organization is to focus all energies, resources, and attention to the fulfillment of a common goal or task.

If organized religion simply organized our corporate hunger, fanned our passion for God like a blacksmith's bellows, and accelerated and aided our pursuit of God, it would be commendable and wholly acceptable. When it turns our focus away from spiritual hunger and the pursuit of God and toward the orderly construction of something else, however, it is neither commendable nor acceptable.

This brings us to another harmful paradigm: the tendency of the cult of "religious decency and man-pleasing order" to smother every ember of God-ward passion or hint of wildfire in the local church. My question is, What if God, the One who openly despises "lukewarm" hearts, lit the fire in our hearts and personally fanned the flames in His house? What—or who—are we trying to "quench" then?[3]

We tend to satisfy our hunger pains through the performance of minor religious duties such as once-a-week church attendance or an occasional prayer on the run. Hunger has ceased to be part of our religious vocabulary because it is considered "undignified" by today's spiritual elite. They don't realize that hunger is among the most attractive things they have to offer to their Creator. (p. 33)

FILLING THE VOID

Add the key words needed to make the following statements true or worthy of serious consideration by biblical standards:

Organization effectively serves the church when it helps us _____ our corporate _____, fan our _____ for ____, and _____ and aid our _____ of God. Organized religion becomes a problem when it turns our _____ away from _____ _____ and the _____ of God and toward the orderly construction of _____ _____.

Hunger may not fit into man's usual definition of decency and order, but it must be _____ to our religious _____ because it is one of the _____ _____ things we have to offer to our _____.

TAKE IT PERSONALLY!

At some point, you need to decide and declare, "Lord, I thank You for what You've done, but I am desperate for what You can do." (p. 34)

Remember Where You've Been, But Always Dare to Dream

That kind of desperation and brokenness can pull God from His hiding place. No wonder He said, "Seek My face." God is just waiting to reveal His face to somebody who is desperate enough and bold enough to pull Him out of hiding.

It is entirely possible and even *desirable* for you to be grateful and desperate at the same time. (pp. 34–35)

I know you want more of Him than you have right now, but just how desperate are you?

1. God is just waiting to reveal His face to somebody. Is that "somebody" you?

2. Are you desperate enough and bold enough to pull Him out of hiding with your brokenness? (You don't have to wait until Sunday morning dawns; the Great Physician has been known to make house calls in desperate situations.)

What Do You Think?

Ezra said the noise of the weepers and the noise of the rejoicers could not be distinguished from each other. I propose that this is the proper posture for the church. *We are grateful for what He has done, but we are also desperate for what He can do.* This odd mix of joy with sorrow, of satisfaction with hunger, is common wherever God shows up. (p. 35)

1. What do you think about this suggested "posture" for the church? Do you think some of our problems (e.g., apathy, division, stagnation) can be caused by the absence of either gratefulness or desperation, joy or sorrow?

2. Have you ever experienced this odd mix in your pursuit of God's face? Describe it.

TAKE IT PERSONALLY!

Perhaps there will be more powerful services when there are more passionate servants. I've really never known of a dry *service*—just dry *servants!* (p. 35)

What Do You Think?

We should be reassured and encouraged when God brings us to the point where we don't know whether to laugh or cry. (p. 35)

What do you think happens in our hearts when we reach the point where we don't know whether to laugh or cry?

❑ We lose confidence in our own strength and ability to direct our lives.
❑ We finally release our death grip on our own agendas and ways of doing things.
❑ (*Fill in your own answer.*)

More Erroneous Assumptions, Presumptions, and Misaligned Paradigms

A holy hunger is being fired up inside you that will take you to the edge of dissatisfaction and joy at the same time . . . Once you reach the point where it is all you can do to maintain your composure, my question is, Why try? When you don't know whether to laugh or cry, you may be in a good place. (p. 36)

Christians in general seem to have an obsession with the erroneous assumption that they must maintain their composure at all costs. Do you see evidence in the life and ministry of Jesus of His always remaining imperturbable? List some examples from the Gospels where people lost their composure or ditched their dignity to receive something from Jesus. (Hint: See Matt. 15:22–28; Mark 2:1–12; 10:46–52; Luke 19:1–10.)

REMEMBER THIS

He is strangely attracted to our desperation and "holy appetite" for His visitation and manifest presence. It all goes back to the heart. (p. 36)

FILLING THE VOID

You need _____ _____ to His Word, His Spirit, and His people, the church. His _____ is literally the air your _____-___ breathes. Jesus wasn't talking just for the fun of it when He _____ _____ the _____ of Life. He is our _____, our _____, our ___, our Rock and Shield, our _____, our _____, our Redeemer, our _____, our Great High Priest, our Advocate. Need I say more? We need Him _____ _____ of every day. To say anything else is _____. (p. 37)

TAKE IT
PERSONALLY!

What I don't see in the New Testament is any command requiring us (or even permitting us) to be complacent, apathetic, or lethargic. (p. 37)

More Erroneous Assumptions, Presumptions, and Misaligned Paradigms

John the disciple was grateful for the Lord's companionship, but his desperate hunger to be closer to Jesus caused him to lay his head on the Lord's chest at every opportunity . . . All he knew was that if the Master was within touching distance, then he would go straight for the heart.

John's "God addiction" isn't something to be scorned; it is something to be sought after and duplicated in our own lives . . .

He was literally caught up into the heavenly scene. He caught God, and God caught him. (p. 39)

In practice, too many Christians seem to agree with the world's negative statement, "Religion is just a crutch for weak people." The false presumption behind this thinking is that it is actually possible for *some* people to be strong enough *not* to need God.

1. What preconditioned response did you feel in your emotions the first time you saw or heard the term *God addiction*?

2. How has your opinion and response changed now that you've discovered the reasoning and basis for the term?

3. Are you "afflicted" with John's God addiction? If not, why not?

TAKE IT
PERSONALLY!

Passionate pursuit has the potential to change your perspective, like a father lifting up his child to give the child a better view. John was lifted above time to get a better view of eternity. (p. 39)

REMEMBER THIS

When you pray with persistence, worship with abandon, or fast in hunger and desperation, you create heavenly urgency and passion that are virtually irresistible to your Maker and heavenly Father. Too many of us miss the mark of passion when we seek the arrival of revival instead of the face of the Reviver. (p. 40)

What Do You Think?

Logic and intellect have their proper place, but it is not in the intimacy of the Holy of Holies. (p. 40)

What do you think?

FILLING THE VOID

Intimacy overrode _____; passion overcame _____. That's the _____ of _____ versus the power of _____. If you are in the _____ of a _____-seeker,[4] your position has _____. (p. 40)

More Erroneous Assumptions, Presumptions, and Misaligned Paradigms

The medical team in the emergency room isn't interested in pointing fingers or placing blame when a person suffers cardiac arrest. The sole objective is to restore heart function before brain function and life itself are lost.

In a sense, God has His church in the spiritual ER, and He is trying to restore heart function to a body that is trying to survive on mere brain function much of the time.

> We must seek Him while He may be found. It doesn't matter whether we begin at His feet with eyes filled with the tears of brokenhearted passion, or move straight to His heart with our whole being in complete surrender and desperation. He responds to the cries of the hungry, but He can't do anything with the complacent requests and halfhearted queries of the satisfied and self-sufficient. (p. 41)

1. Patients suffering cardiac arrest often appear groggy and give halfhearted replies to medical personnel. At other times they adamantly demand to be released because "they are perfectly fine." Compare these characteristics to this quote from *The God Catchers*.

2. How about you? Are you seeking Him more through your head than through your heart?

(Both routes lead to Him, but intellect often functions more as a roadblock to be overcome than as an expressway to speed progress toward the destination.)

REMEMBER THIS

I think we've become too familiar with the pleasure of His provisions and the blessings of His hand. We've forsaken the tears of repentance and passionate desperation known by the revered saints of the past. It is time to rediscover the power of passionate and fervent prayer. (p. 41)

What Do You Think?

I am tired of endless church meetings and the constant buzz of man's activity in the name of God. I'm desperate for Him. He is the One I fell in love with—all the other things just get in the way of my pursuit of Him. (pp. 41–42)

What do you think?

TAKE IT PERSONALLY!

He made it clear that His chief interest is in your desperation, hunger, and passion for His presence. *He is not after performance; He wants passion.*

Remember that when passion reenters the church, His presence comes back through the door as well. (p. 43)

NOTES

NOTES

4

SHALL WE GATHER AT THE RIVER OR JUST JUMP IN?

THE PERILS OF VALUING PROGRAM ABOVE PRESENCE

There is only one way to avoid the error of the priests on the day of the triumphant entry: at some point we must get desperately hungry for Him. Shall we just gather at the river? I say we jump in! The promised land is waiting! (p. 59)

Fear keeps most non-swimmers out of the water, and it keeps most religious people out of the waters of faith as well. This most basic of human emotions is the foundation of our irrational dislike of *change*. You probably know people who will do almost anything to avoid or hinder changes in their daily routines, business plans, religious rituals, and relationships.

Fear and its twin sister in the spirit realm, unbelief, combine to doom many good people to the tomb of yesterday's accomplishments. Unfortunately, the dreams God gave them for today and tomorrow also get buried in the pit of fear as well.

The truth is that much vital growth in the Christian life takes place through the faith-stretching process of change and challenge. Whether we like it or not, the greatest things in God's kingdom can only be achieved or acquired through faith—the process that takes us beyond our comfort zone and into God's supernatural provision and direction. (In other words, faith demands a calculated risk based on the faithfulness of God.)

What Do You Think?

I didn't see any use in "gathering" at the river if I couldn't float on it, fish in it, cross it, or jump in for a refreshing swim. I never really understood the songs we used to sing until I met the One we were singing about. I wonder how long, in our collective immaturity, we have sung about His presence without ever diving in? (p. 46)

1. What do you think? How many times—or how many years—have you sung about entering His presence without even sensing it, let alone "diving in"? How desperate are you to experience the Real Thing?

2. What do you think? Did all of this talk about "His presence" begin to make more sense after you experienced your first encounter with God's manifest presence, or are you still waiting for that encounter?

Erroneous Assumptions, Presumptions, and Misaligned Paradigms

Yet the fact is that *rivers are to cross and transition through.* The Israelites in the wilderness chose to embrace all the negative reports and the "safe" counsel of men instead of the "riskier" counsel of God. As a result, an entire generation died homeless. They never stepped into the water of transition from the deliverance of bondage to the possession of God's promise. It's time for this generation to dive into the river. (p. 46)

1. For centuries, the church has viewed the twin rivers of "change and challenge" as obstacles to be avoided and enemies to be feared. Can you name specific instances in your life where a local church has stalled at the river of challenge and failed to cross into God's blessings through unbelief or fear?

2. What command of God to individuals or entire congregations does not include a commission to change and a call to meet a challenge? Given a choice, will most people embrace change and tackle a challenge or escape change and sidestep a challenge?

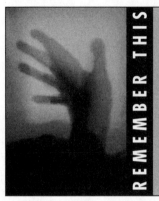

REMEMBER THIS

There is nothing wrong with stained glass or well-trained choirs, and preaching is obviously a thoroughly biblical foundation of the Christian life. However, I don't mean to burst a cherished bubble, but God isn't impressed with any of these things. *They are for us,* not Him. He comes to our meetings only in response to our worship and our hunger. (p. 47)

What Do You Think?

Remember that earthly brokenness creates heavenly openness. For that reason, I am compelled by the Spirit of God to make what may be one of the oddest statements you will ever see in a Christian book:

Don't let church obscure your view of God. (p. 47)

1. What do you think? Does "church" (in the man-centered format) tend to foster earthly brokenness or earthly self-sufficiency?

2. What do you think? Is it true that whatever "opens the heavens" would clarify your view of God, and that whatever "closes the heavens" obscures the view of divinity? Explain.

More Erroneous Assumptions, Presumptions, and Misaligned Paradigms

The Holy Spirit is pointing to the coming of the Father in all His glory, and we are still scrabbling in the parking lot, digging for religious paving stones to say, "Look . . ." Religion causes us to gather together for all the wrong reasons. (p. 48)

1. The misaligned paradigm of my daughter in the parking lot at the Grand Canyon overlook was that her focus was aimed downward. She missed the big picture she *could not* see (from the parking lot) in her zeal to explore the little picture she *could* see. Do you get the feeling the church is missing the big picture too? Explain.

2. If religion calls us together for a "parking lot party," what is the "right reason" to gather together?

TAKE IT PERSONALLY!

Sinners hear countless stories on the news and in the local barber and beauty shops about Christian people who gather to debate the commands of God and come to verbal blows over meaningless jots and tittles while shoving aside the most important things. (p. 48)

Take this personally. Remember—the world is watching and listening, just hoping that God might actually show up in us.

What Do You Think?

We want equations and formulas, the stuff and structure of man's programs. Even at our best, when somehow we align our hearts with the heart of God and He visits us for a moment, we instinctively grope for a formula to re-create it. The desire for more is godly, but the methodology is not. (p. 49)

What do you think? Is this true or not? Explain, using examples from your life and experience.

FILLING THE VOID

This passage is longer than most, but it contains more truth than most as well. Find the original passage on page 48 and fill in the void where necessary. (There is a significant point behind this exercise—the missing words often point to discrepancies or problem areas that can seriously affect our efforts to pursue the face of God.)

Like my little daughter cradling those worthless rocks in the parking lot of the Grand Canyon, we carefully _____ our _____ and reluctantly place it at His feet as if it were of _____ value. Yet we are merely offering God "_____ _____" from His golden streets instead of placing our _____ on His _____—the true source of all _____ and _____ in the kingdom.

God has to break through our _____ before He can _____ ____ and manifest His _____ among us. He has to demolish our artificial _____ (our dim and sometimes haughty imitation of His _____) and artificial _____ (our programs) to bring in the _____ _____ and take a city or nation.

Unfortunately it is a rare _____ that can handle the divine call to self-_____ and _____ by the _____ of God . . . That means we have to face a "garden of _____" experience *before* we can see His _____.

Once you have written in the missing answers, reread this passage, and let its meaning sink deeper into your spirit. Are you willing to accept the call to spiritual demolition and reignition?

TAKE IT
PERSONALLY!

God will move the door to the secret place and change the point of access so that His relationship with you doesn't become an empty ritual commemorating what once was. He wants to preserve the joy and freshness of our encounters together, and equations and formulas do exactly the opposite. (p. 49)

More Erroneous Assumptions, Presumptions, and Misaligned Paradigms

God wants to "break outside of the box." That means that our hunger has to get bigger than the religious box we've built over multiplied centuries of man-centered religious practice. We must have an *uncontainable hunger* to entertain our *uncontainable God*. That automatically disqualifies the religious program. By definition, a program is a prepackaged, manageable, predictable reproduction of what worked once for somebody somewhere. But God doesn't do "out of the box revival." (p. 50)

Apparently the modern church has a fixed paradigm or set of assumptions about "revival" that appears nowhere in the Scriptures. Even a casual comparison between modern "revival" as practiced today and revival by biblical standards as revealed in the Scriptures and church history unveils some telling differences. Examine these comparisons and *you decide* which pattern is rooted in biblical truth:

- Philip the evangelist was sent out to preach the gospel *to the lost*. *[a]* This is impossible today. How could he support a family by ministering solely to the lost? It is unrealistic because the church would actually have to support him and send him out. *[b]* Yes, this is the biblical pattern; and yes, the church is *supposed* to send out and support evangelists in the New Testament pattern.

- Modern evangelists spend most of their time preaching to the saved, evidently in continuous attempts to revive what has died. When they do encounter unsaved people, many are so religious in language and appearance that they have no common ground upon which to share a relevant gospel. *[a]* This is false. Most evangelistic crusades see lots of people saved in their meetings held in churches. The lost can't wait to enter our church buildings, copy our dress styles, learn our special church language, and conform to all of our rules of conduct *so that they can be saved*. *[b]* This is true, although a few people still manage to get saved in such meetings by the providence and supernatural intervention of God.

- Revival in the book of Acts affected entire families, cities and regions (such as Asia Minor), often took place in the streets or public meeting places, brought thousands of disciples to Christ at one time, and never included an offering to pay expenses. *[a]* I know this is in the Bible, but it is a work of fiction in modern society. Nobody is reaching entire families or cities in our day, so it can't be done. Besides, who ever heard of having a revival without taking offerings—lots of offerings—with really *big* buckets. *[b]* This is true, but it takes an outpouring of God's presence that is rare in our day. The only way to see it happen again is for God's presence to visit us again. As for the offerings, the church should underwrite every effort to make disciples in the city, the region, and the world.

Revival comes when the Father shows up and man shows up at the same time and same place and a supernatural encounter occurs in which "God and man are sat down." Anytime we try to program it, we automatically make the thing too small for God to fit into it. (p. 50)

What Do You Think?

We have the unfortunate habit of offering worship to the instrument instead of to the divine Player of the earthly instrument. And I read somewhere that "no flesh should glory in His presence."[1] I take that warning very seriously. (p. 51)

1. What do you think? Do people tend to worship or overly exalt people who are powerfully used by God?

2. What do you think? Who bears the blame for it? The people who offer the excessive praise, or the spiritual leaders who accept it or even encourage it?

I no longer attend church meetings to minister to people; *I go to minister to Him.* Ever since He touched me, I go to every church meeting, worship service, and prayer gathering, saying, "I wonder if this will be the night He will show up again?" (p. 51)

More Erroneous Assumptions, Presumptions, and Misaligned Paradigms

I don't know if that is where you live, but I am desperately hungry for an outbreak of God. I am like millions of other people around the world who are nauseated by the brand of spectator Christianity that dominates our spiritual landscape. Our modern form of "wisdom" and heightened appetite for entertainment have overtaken the church. We've turned the worship service into a polished performance that entices the soul and fluffs the flesh (while doing nothing for the only One worthy of true worship). (p. 52)

Jesus once rebuked some learned spiritual leaders and scholars with this unusual statement: "Ye do err, not knowing the scriptures" (Matt. 22:29 KJV). One problem is that we don't stop to examine our ways and methods in the light of God's Word.

1. In your opinion, how would "spectator Christianity" nauseate a genuine God Chaser?

2. What is missing when you focus on "enticing the soul" and "fluffing the flesh" while neglecting to truly worship God?

What Do You Think?

The best thing we can do is to discard our programs, shred our syllabi, slide off our pews, and fall on our knees. (p. 52)

What do you think?

REMEMBER THIS

I think God's brand of church splits the heavens wide open and opens a window of glorious access between God and man. It releases such power that it starts New Testament churches and re-creates the joy, the ecstasy, and the sound and fury that the 120 experienced in the Upper Room in Jerusalem on pentecost two thousand years ago. (pp. 53–54)

FILLING THE VOID

We want the _____ _____ for revival, the "____-_____ presence" version supposedly produced if you mix just the right _____ with just the right _____ and a liberal dose of _____ to raise the people's emotions.

. . . Too many of us are content with the tried and proven ways of man, where we _____ ____ ____ into His presence with _____ shows of _____ and a secret intention of human _____. We are happy if He just sticks His hands out from _____ the veil to distribute our _____ _____ of wants, desires, and pleasant spiritual gifts. (p. 54)

More Erroneous Assumptions, Presumptions, and Misaligned Paradigms

God is restless to break out in this generation, and He will do it *in spite of us* if He has to. If we fail to discard our man-programs and make room for Him in our churches, then He will break out in barrooms. In fact, God shows a peculiar liking for the kind of spiritual hunger that shows up *outside* the buildings we think are so holy. (p. 55)[2]

We assume too much if we believe God will work only through the established churches to bring revival to the land. Think about the events that took place in Jesus' day involving the religious establishment and what happened when most of the Jewish religious world rejected the Messiah in that era. What does that say to the Christian religious establishment today?

Dig Deeper

(MINING FOR GOLD IN THE FINE PRINT OF THE ENDNOTES)

My opinion is that any church that offers the Real Thing has nothing to fear from those who offer poor substitutes.

I think we should stop throwing rocks at the New Age Movement and offer them *bread* instead—the *bread of His presence*.[10] (p. 56)

FILLING THE VOID

There is gold stored in the endnotes of *The God Catchers*. The endnote for this passage is especially important. Dig deeper until you find endnote 10 on page 198, and fill in the void as appropriate:

The term "_____ of His _____" is explained in this brief passage from my book, *The God Chasers,* Chapter 2: "No Bread in the 'House of Bread,'" p. 19: "_____ has always been the one thing historically that was an indicator of His _____. We find in the Old Testament that bread in the form of _____ was in the _____ _____. It was called 'the _____ of the _____' (Num. 4:7 NRSV). Showbread might better be interpreted as '_____ ___ bread,' or in the Hebraic terms, '_____ bread.' It was a heavenly symbol of God Himself."

What Do You Think?

If you are going to make fun of New Age people, then you also should make fun of the starving children in Somalia and Ethiopia as well.

These movements are merely indicators of the spiritual hunger that exists in the world. They indicate something else as well. It is proof that the church in its present state has not been able to meet that spiritual hunger. (p. 56)

What do you think?

REMEMBER THIS

Let me say it again: anyone who has a genuine encounter with the manifested glory of God won't have to ask, "Is it really Him?" (p. 57)

More Erroneous Assumptions, Presumptions, and Misaligned Paradigms

If we are not careful, we can lock ourselves inside our church traditions, agendas, programs, and empty rituals praying for Him to come while He passes by outside our religious box! We can easily miss our moment of visitation if He doesn't come in the format that we think He should! (It is almost certain that He will.) (p. 59)

Presumption may be one of our most dangerous enemies! Presumption causes us to assume that God thinks as we do when the facts are that He doesn't, and any intelligence we may think we have is on loan from God anyway. Fill in the "presumption blanks" as appropriate:

1. Presumption says, "Of course God likes the kind of music I like—we've sung these songs for as _____ as I can _____. Even Paul the apostle and Peter liked these songs. That's why we always sing _____ of them before we take up the _____ and make _____. Then we turn it over to the _____."

2. You can't "have church" unless the preacher _____. It's ungodly.

3. Of course we need to make announcements during the service. It's the way we've _____ _____ it. It's in the Bible, isn't it?

4. When revival comes, we'll be all _____ up and in our favorite _____ at the _____ building like always. I sure hope He visits on _____ morning though; I've got plans during the evenings.

5. Of course God will visit _____ first. We've been praying for revival in our _____. Why would He want to go somewhere else? We've paid our spiritual _____ more than the other churches, so we _____ it more than they do.

(Just in case you aren't versed in the basic "religious traditions" that seem to permeate many evangelical Protestant churches in North America, here is the "Presumption Answer Key" to these statements: (1) long, remember, three, offering, announcements, preacher or pastor; (2) preaches; (3) always done; (4) dressed, pew or seat, church, Sunday; (5) here, church, dues, deserve.)

NOTES

. . . .

. . . .

. . . .

. . . .

. . . .

. . . .

. . . .

. . . .

. . . .

NOTES

NOTES

5

WHEN DESTINY MEETS DESPERATION

NO MORE JESUS PARADES

Father, we draw a line in the sand; we'll never be the same.
We are hungry for You, and we cannot go back; we refuse to retreat
to the closet of fear from the place of public passion. (p. 73)

If fear is the problem, then desperate hunger and burning passion for God are the cure. In my experience, I've noticed that genuine hunger can help us overcome almost any fear, dislike, or discomfort. I'm convinced that God often gives us just enough "rope" to reach the end of our strength and natural sources of supply. It is there, in the place of desperation and the bankruptcy of our abilities, that destiny can have her perfect work and plant us squarely in the purposes of God.

Remember Where You've Been, But Always Dare to Dream

Have you noticed that true hunger has an uncanny ability to make us genuinely real and brutally honest? Just the mention of the word *hunger* recalls the mental picture of a hungry baby who thinks nothing of disrupting a church service to display his hunger. (p. 62)

1. When you think of the word *hunger,* what image fills your mind?

2. Have you ever been hungry—hungry to the point of desperation or even starvation? Do you think spiritual hunger can reach the same desperation point?

3. Recall times of spiritual hunger in your life (perhaps it is more than a mere memory—you may be desperately hungry for Him right now). What are you prepared to do about it?

What Do You Think?

Some of us have "faked fullness" for most of our Christian lives. Whether in church or on the job, we live with a pasted-on smile, and we refuse to leave home without it. The truth is that more and more Christian "fakers of fullness" are saying, "I've had enough of that." Their inner hunger is beginning to get the best of them, and God is beginning to get interested once again. (p. 63)

1. What do you think? Are you personally acquainted with "faked fullness" and the pasted-on smile? Explain.

2. Being totally honest with yourself, is your inner hunger beginning to get the best of you? Describe what is happening in your life as you learn more about hunger and the pursuit of God.

Erroneous Assumptions, Presumptions, and Misaligned Paradigms

A deep conviction is overtaking the church—an inner knowing is growing that something is terribly wrong. We spend entire lifetimes sitting in pews but leave the four walls of our churches and make no impact on our world whatsoever. We hear sermon after sermon, countless Bible teachings, and audit hundreds of hours of vocal specials, but we still wonder if we know Him. (p. 63)

One of the most damaging misaligned paradigms in the Christian world is the idea that church is attending meetings and hearing sermons and Bible teachings. It can be confusing because we are supposed to receive training, encouragement, and correction through the preaching and teaching of God's Word. The problem is that we begin to think, *That is all there is.* No, there's more.

1. Can you estimate how many sermons you've heard in your lifetime?

2. How many Bible studies or classes have you attended in your life?

3. What stands out in your memory as an event or experience that you know brought you significantly closer to God?

(For most of us, it was *not* a sermon, a lesson, or a song. It was a personal encounter with Him, no matter how brief it was.)

TAKE IT
PERSONALLY!

It's simple: God's children need more than Daddy's Word, Daddy's gifts, Daddy's daily provision, or the assistance of Daddy's earthly assistants. We need Him. We desperately long to feel His touch on our lives. (p. 64)

What Do You Think?

"No, nothing is more important to Me than preplanning encounters with My children." Then He added, "I can't make Zacchaeus climb the tree, but I can plant the tree. Only his hunger will cause him to climb the tree. In the meantime, My sovereignty will make sure the tree is in its place, ready and waiting for his climb to destiny." (p. 65)

1. What do you think? Do you believe God really wants to have encounters with people? Do you believe God has planted "a tree of destiny" for you? Have you already climbed it?

2. If you haven't encountered your "tree" yet, how hungry are you? What will you do when you find the tree God prepared for you?

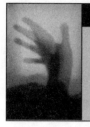

REMEMBER THIS

Don't miss your moment in the Son; God has invested more than you know in you and your encounter with Him. (p. 65)

TAKE IT
PERSONALLY!

How many times could your destiny have been short-circuited but for the providence of the Father? I read that He has made plans for you, and they are good, not evil. (p. 67)

FILLING THE VOID

When humanity _____ _____ of the glory of God, He planted _____ _____ of inestimable worth. The tree of _____ for the rest of us was _____ on the top of _____, and ___ _____ climbed it first so it would still be standing on our ___ of _____. We can't see Him from ___ _____ vantage point, but if we can just _____ that tree, we'll transcend _____ and access His _____ _____ for eternity. (p. 66)

More Erroneous Assumptions, Presumptions, and Misaligned Paradigms

Some people may feel that they can satisfy their hunger by watching from the sidelines and patting their children on the shoulder as they point to the parade to say, "That's Him. Watch Him now as He passes by. Never forget this moment." Hunger humbled me and consumed me until I had to find a way to get more of Him than I had. A passing glimpse would not do. I had to touch something, even if it was the hem of His garment. (p. 67)

We are now at least two generations into the "TV era," and we are finding it difficult to tell the difference between fantasy on the screen and reality right in front of us! Take this Spectator Christian Quiz to see if you are a parade watcher or a parade stopper:

1. When I go to church, I . . .
   ❏ a. always wait for my favorite songs to start worshiping God.
   ❏ b. begin worshiping Him when I wake up and just pick up the pace as I meet with other believers for corporate worship.

2. I just don't feel that I've "had church" unless . . .
   ❏ a. I see the pastor step behind the pulpit and preach.
   ❏ b. we keep worshiping and ministering to Him until His manifested presence comes in some way.

3. When I leave a church service, I want to feel . . .

❑ a. satisfied and comfortable enough to hold out for another week.

❑ b. hungrier for God's presence than when I came, and even more aware of my desperate love and need for Him.

4. I never feel complete in a service unless . . .

❑ a. I've received some blessing from God.

❑ b. I've somehow given Him something more of myself in the way of love, worship, commitment, repentance, or my own brokenness and desperate need for Him.

(Answer key: If you consistently selected "a" answers, you may be wearing a Spectator-brand Christianette suit and have probably attended too many services that were all about us instead of all about Him. If you consistently selected "b" answers, then you are probably "ruined" for church as we know it and are ripe for an encounter with the Object of your passion.)

What Do You Think?

If Bartimaeus had listened to his friends, he would have missed his divine appointment. One cry wasn't enough. Most of us don't like living in the tension between the first cry and God's final response . . . If the first voice that reaches you after your first cry of hunger says, "Calm down," it probably won't be the voice of God.

The truth is that Bartimaeus's friends couldn't do for him what Jesus could. They were offended by the beggar's cries because they perceived the cries to be a distraction; but the Son of God was attracted to Bartimaeus's cries because He perceived them to be worship served on a platter of pure passion. (p. 69)

1. What do you think I mean by "the tension between the first cry and God's final response"? Have you experienced it? Explain.

2. Has your hunger for God distracted or disturbed your friends? Are there people around you who urge you to "calm down" and "be quiet" in your chase for His face? (Do you listen to your heart or their complaints?)

REMEMBER THIS

Jesus is still stopping parades to answer the cries of blind and hungry beggars *(but He never stops for the proud).* (p. 70)

What Do You Think?

There may be times in your life when your spiritual "senses" seem deafened or blinded, and you won't be able to sense the nearness of God. In times of spiritual sensory deprivation, you must walk by faith and stand on His Word. You may have to take someone else's word that He is in the house. Whether it is a worship leader, a spouse, or a preacher, pay close attention when the person says, "He's close." (p. 71)

1. What do you think? It should be obvious that none of us are privileged to live in His manifest presence every day or even in every service. That means we must learn to walk by faith and not by sight. What do you do when you can't sense God's nearness?

2. Describe an experience when God used someone else to help lead you to Him.

More Erroneous Assumptions, Presumptions, and Misaligned Paradigms

Never underestimate the power of one moment in His presence. *Thirty seconds in the manifest presence of God turned a murderer named Saul into a martyr named Paul.* (p. 71)

Many Christians erroneously assume that it takes a long time to experience a lifelong change in habits or lifestyle. When they encounter a problem or obstacle, they assume the posture of suffering or accept the supposed fate of the genes and prepare to live with their problem. If you are battling a problem, whether it is physical, spiritual, financial, mental, or social, insert it in the following declaration, and declare it:

If thirty seconds in the manifest presence of God could change a murderer named Saul into a martyr named Paul, then God's manifest presence could also change my *(place your problem or challenge here)* in just thirty seconds or less.

Any way you look at it, wouldn't it be better to be in His presence than to be anywhere else?

TAKE IT
PERSONALLY!

With all the passion, hunger, and desperation in his being, the son of Timaeus arrested the attention of God the Son. *Radical praise brings radical presence!* (p. 71)

What Do You Think?

Worship comes in many forms. It can touch Him through the slightest brush of a finger against the hem of a garment. It can reach Him through the hoarse-voiced cry of the vocal cords, or it can traverse time and space without a sound as a silent scream of passionate desperation from a broken heart.

. . . Desperate worship stops God in His tracks no matter what social strata it comes from. All are equal in His sight. If God would stop the parade of the universe long enough to change these two human destinies forever, what could He do for you? (p. 72)

1. What do you think? Do you really believe that your desperate worship could actually "stop God"?

2. Reread the passage and answer question 1 again (or as many times as it takes until your answer is yes).

More Erroneous Assumptions, Presumptions, and Misaligned Paradigms

I wish more of us in the church would get tired of standing on the sidewalk of spectator Christianity while the "Jesus parade" goes by. Somebody needs to get hungry enough to cry out. Somebody needs to get desperate enough to arrest the attention of heaven and say, "I'm not going to let You pass me by, Lord. I thank You for what You *have* done, but I'm desperate for what You *can* do." (p. 72)

Another dangerous assumption is that it is up to God to do everything in our lives. Examine the encounters between Jesus and other people. He did His part, but He expected others to do their part:

1. Jesus walked by, but Bartimaeus _____ out to Him.

2. Jesus passed through the crowds, but the woman with the issue of blood _____ out and _____ the hem of His garment.

3. Jesus walked under the sycamore tree in Jericho, but Zacchaeus had to _____ it.

4. Jesus was willing to heal the man with the withered hand, but the man had to _____ it out toward Him.

5. Jesus died on the cross for you, but He expects you to _____ Him as Lord and Savior. Then He requires you to _____ yourself, take up your _____ daily, and _____ Him.

Are you hungry enough to cry out? Are you desperate enough to arrest the attention of heaven?

REMEMBER THIS

God plants the tree in your life, but hunger makes you climb it. God creates the occasion, but you must take advantage of it . . . If you dare to climb the tree of hunger, you may not have to invite Him—He may just invite Himself. (p. 72)

NOTES

NOTES

6

WHAT DOES A HUMAN WAITER OFFER A DIVINE CUSTOMER?

WAITING IN CAFE HEAVEN IS NOT SPIRITUAL THUMB TWIDDLING

He will move heaven and earth for worshipers, skilled waiters who know how to anticipate His needs and satisfy His hunger. Can you imagine being "tipped" by God? Even His spare change can alter your future. (p. 88)

I f you have ever waited on tables, this chapter of *The God Catchers* probably made perfect sense to you. If you've spent most of your adult days clinging to the belief that table waiting and restaurant work is beneath you, I can only hope that the Holy Spirit can help you understand the concept of serving and *waiting* on God.

Perhaps the most helpful point I can offer you, regardless of your background, is that Jesus Christ Himself chose to call Himself a servant. It was Jesus who personally took a waiter's towel in hand and *served* His disciples. Should we do any less in our service to Him?

Erroneous Assumptions, Presumptions, and Misaligned Paradigms

A lot of Christians never "get it" . . . They think church is about them, so they turn church into glorified "bless me clubs" when God thinks it's a "bless *Him* club." (p. 76)

For some reason, God actually thinks people dress up and gather together in a church meeting for *Him!* That gives new meaning to the phrase "waiting on the Lord," doesn't it? (p. 77)

Perhaps the most selfish presumption we make as Christians is that the Cross has become some kind of discount shopper's card at God's warehouse— the place where we can go to pick up the blessings of God's hand with no regard or need to seek God's face. "After all," we reason, "wasn't it all taken care of on the cross?"

Jesus took all of our sins upon Himself at Calvary, but He would never condone the idea that we cease to seek God's face in the name of grace! Take a moment to select an answer to these questions in the light of the revelation that *church is really all about Him:*

1. If church is really all about Him, the time I spend preparing my heart is [more] or [less] important than the time I spend preparing my clothes and physical body.

2. If church is really all about Him, then I should look at my watch [more] or [less] often during worship services.

3. If church is really all about Him, then I should be [more] or [less] concerned about getting my blessings than in becoming a blessing to God.

What Do You Think?

Gifted waiters don't act as if you inconvenienced them by showing up in their restaurant or in their serving section. They make you feel special, as if you are a long-lost and beloved family member who has returned for a special reunion meal . . .

Can I tell you that is also what a good worship "service" is like? The Lord loves to come to services where we anticipate His every desire and whim. He delights to see us carefully seek the guidance of the Holy Spirit in every part of the service—whether our preset song lists, order of service, or programs are disrupted or not. (p. 78)

1. What do you think? Is it really possible to make God feel special, like a beloved family member being honored at a reunion meal? (Hint: See 1 Cor. 11:23–26.)

2. What do you think? How often have you attended a worship service in which every effort was made to "seek the guidance of the Holy Spirit," even if it meant changing previously made plans? Was the service significantly different from other services? Explain.

TAKE IT PERSONALLY!

If we forget that this is all about Him, if we revert to the myth that church is all about us, then we never quite enter in and we miss the whole purpose of it all. The short version of this is that we need a perspective change. (p. 79)

More Erroneous Assumptions, Presumptions, and Misaligned Paradigms

An elevated perspective changes everything.

That is why you can come into a worship service weighed down with big troubles and insurmountable problems and suddenly sense a change the moment you catch an "updraft" of the Spirit . . . Suddenly you find yourself soaring in His presence. When you take time to look down, the childlike part of you wants to turn to Him in awe and wonder to say, "Wook, Daddy! Widdle troubles, widdle problems, widdle fears." (pp. 80–81)

Some of the most common assumptions or misaligned paradigms are those we cling to individually. They are rarely voiced or supported by the leadership in our churches, but these ideas and ways of thinking persist. None is more common than the "mountain of a problem" paradigm.

Can you count the times you've entered a worship service with your thoughts clouded and overshadowed by a pressing problem or mountain of fear and doubt? (If it has happened more times than you can count, then you are like most Christians today.) This may well point to:

a. an earthbound mentality.

b. a form of spiritual myopia (nearsightedness) that afflicts every believer at some time or another.

c. a habit of looking harder and longer at the problem than at the face of God and His unchanging Word.

d. a need for a new perspective, preferably from the heavenly realm of God.

e. all of the above.

FILLING THE VOID

Your _____ aren't too big—*perhaps your _____ is too small. How ____ are your problems? It is time to "_____ your _____"* in His presence and ____ above them. If you can ascend _____ _____, your problems become _____ and are less _____. Why? Your heavenly Father never _____ for you to dwell in the earthly realm, constantly _____ __ and _____ __ your problems. You were _____ for the _____. (p. 81)

I said, "God, what are You trying to teach me?" That was when He whispered to me, *If you can _____ man whom you ____ see, there is a potential to _____ God, whom you _____ see.* (p. 84)

What Do You Think?

What will happen if we ever learn how to entertain His presence by waiting on Him? Is there any way to measure the potential of the supernatural power of God released in His people? *If a city is to receive divine visitation, someone must learn how to host the Holy Spirit!* (p. 84)

What do you think?

TAKE IT PERSONALLY!

The only way we can break free from the stressing restraints of time is to put our full trust in the eternal God who lives outside the circle of time. (p. 85)

More Erroneous Assumptions, Presumptions, and Misaligned Paradigms

Everybody likes the end results of a miracle, but no one likes the waiting process. Yet it is in the waiting that He actually proves He is God in response to your absolute dependency on Him. (p. 86)

Time is a matter of perspective. Whenever we settle down in the presence of God, we find strength to stand because we are connected to the One who holds eternity in His hand. (p. 87)

Another presumption that promotes folly is the idea that time spent waiting on God is time wasted. There is something about waiting that makes us feel helpless or ineffective. If God really didn't exist, then perhaps impatience would be a virtue, but it might lead to man helping himself. The truth is that God does exist, and therefore, patience is the virtue, and impatience is generally an act of unbelief or disobedience.

What are some rewards of "waiting on God"?

1. You will never be _____ (see Ps. 25:3).

2. The God of your salvation will ____ you in _____ and teach you (see Ps. 25:5).

3. Integrity and _____ will _____ you (see Ps. 25:21).

4. God will _____ your heart (see Ps. 27:14).

5. You will _____ the earth (see Ps. 37:9).

6. God will _____ you (see Ps. 37:34).

7. God will _____ your strength; you will _____ __ with wings like eagles, you will ___ and not be _____, you will ____ and not faint (see Isa. 40:31).

REMEMBER THIS

Remember that worship is the process of finding and being found. It is the progression of discovering His presence and of experiencing His reactive joy over being discovered! (p. 88)

FILLING THE VOID

If you come to Him _____, He will _____ you. If you come to Him _____, He will _____ you; but He will give you only _____ for _____. You must seek Him for _____ tomorrow. His presence is _____ that must be sought and received _____ _____ ____ lest it become stale. We've made a religion out of living on dried-out crumbs from yesterday's foray into His presence. (p. 88)

What Do You Think?

We know from the Divine Record that by the time heaven's fire fell on the worshipers in the Upper Room and "set their hair on fire," there were 120 people in the room. *What happened to the other 380 people?* They just couldn't wait. When you can't wait, you may miss your moment. (p. 89)

1. What do you think? What do you think happened to the "other 380"?

2. How far will you go to make sure you don't miss your moment?

Remember Where You've Been,
But Always Dare to Dream

Our problem is that we get in such an all-fired hurry to get results that we try to use man's matches to set our own hair on fire! *There is a big difference between the fire of God and the fire of man.* When the fire of God's presence descends to the earthly realm, it burns but doesn't consume . . .

On the other hand, a lot of people have been burned by "the church in a hurry" over the centuries. Man's fire promotes man's methods instead of God's purpose and presence. That's why we often experience "burnout." (p. 90)

1. Do you have "singed hair" and "burn scars" from man's fire and man's methods? Explain.

2. In your opinion, do people get burned in the church when leaders wait on God too long, or when they grow too impatient to wait and try to light a holy fire themselves?

REMEMBER THIS

You know men are reaching in their own pockets for matches when their words indicate the presence of a fleshly clock somewhere:

"Is this service going somewhere? We need to *do something*. I just wish we'd hurry up and get to the point."

He is the point. His presence is the destination.

"Well, what are we going to *do?* What's next?"

That is like standing on top of Mount Everest and saying, "Which way is up?" *One step in any direction is a step down.* (p. 90)

More Erroneous Assumptions, Presumptions, and Misaligned Paradigms

Time and time again I watch people worship and welcome God until His manifest presence enters their meetings—and then some of them begin to look at their watches, consult their order of service, or glance at their sermon notes and say, "Well, we've got to continue on with the program now."

What program? I thought this was all about Him!

. . . We need to learn how to revere divine interruptions. (p. 90)

When the manifest presence of God enters a worship service, human timetables and man-made agendas often lose all value. In that moment, we must either revere the divine interruption or despise it as a mere disruption of the established order. Everything that follows will depend on that decision. The problem is:

1. Divine interruptions nearly always require the dismantling of human programs. True or false?

2. When God's manifest presence enters center stage, there is no longer any room for man to share the spotlight. True or false?

3. Those seeking man's approval must deal with feelings of jealousy when God enters a service and draws all hearts to Himself. (After all, didn't they labor over their sermons and songs for many hours? How can they just "lay them down" in the absence of any plan, program, or sequence of preestablished events?) True or false?

4. The God who created time is under no obligation to complete His work by lunchtime. (Doesn't God know those roasts we have cooking at home are expensive?) True or false?

What Do You Think?

Sometimes our greatest temptations for interrupting God's divine disruptions are rooted in some of God's best gifts . . .

We are so *blessed* by God's Word and by His leaders and charismatic gifts that we can quickly forget that church is about Him, not us . . . God's gifts should never, ever, in no way whatsoever, take away or minimize our service of love to *Him*. Our primary object of pursuit should be the Giver, not the gifts! (p. 91)

To some people, this kind of talk borders on blasphemy. Is there a New Testament precedent or example demonstrating the proper attitude of church leaders toward God's divine interruption of worship or planned ministry? (Hint: See what John the Baptist said when his anointed ministry was interrupted by divinity in John 3:25–31.) What do you think?

TAKE IT PERSONALLY!

To interrupt the ongoing visitation of God just to maintain a program is to step off the crest of Mount Everest so you can read a mountain-climbing manual or receive instructions on how to "reach the top." It is nothing short of a step down from the best. (p. 92)

More Erroneous Assumptions, Presumptions, and Misaligned Paradigms

The pregnancy stage of revival involves waiting and worshiping. If you have made a good beginning, do not let the pregnancy of purpose turn into a miscarriage of man or an abortion . . .

What does a human waiter offer a divine customer? You offer Him good "service"! Offer Him persistent worship and insistent hunger that refuse to give up until He shows up, not spiritual thumb twiddling! (pp. 93–94)

For years, many churches have operated under the assumption that "revival" happens when you arrange for a revivalist to show up, hype up, and light up the gospel fireworks for an extended period of three days or even two weeks. As I noted elsewhere, revival is when God and man show up at the same place and the same time. It is when human hunger attracts and collides with the fire of divine presence. Man has nothing to do with the timing or the fire—all we can bring to the table is our hunger and desperation for Him. He is the exclusive Supply for everything else. If there is such a thing as a checklist, then it might look like this:

1. If He supplies the fireworks, that means He has no need for
   ❏ human hype.
   ❏ man's methods or man's management.
   ❏ man's impatience-driven rush to rapid results and quick delivery of God's presence.
   ❏ self-appointed firemen with stacks of wet blankets determined to put out wildfires of passion for God and self-abandonment in His presence.

2. The key ingredients for revival are
   ❏ the manifested presence of the Reviver.
   ❏ displayed hunger and desperation.
   ❏ the irresistible service and fragrance of true worship and praise for God.

3. If you want to experience encounters with God's manifest presence
   ❏ offer persistent worship.
   ❏ demonstrate and display insistent hunger.
   ❏ stubbornly refuse to give up until He shows up.

Remember Where You've Been, But Always Dare to Dream

Everybody is "a little bit pitiful" in the sense that we all have our places and points of pain. If we can learn to turn our obstacles into altars and worship through the night when necessary, then God will show up in His manifested glory in the middle of it. (p. 95)

The passionate pursuit of God is more than a nice idea for sunny days when everything is going well. It is our destiny and our surest path to peace and security in the worst of times. If you are alive, then you will experience pain and difficulty. The solution isn't pain avoidance, but pain openly displayed and embraced in His presence:

1. The woman with the _____ of _____ pressed through the crowd to touch the hem of Jesus' garment. He stopped the Jesus parade just to meet the one among hundreds whose desperation tapped the fountain of His healing virtue (Mark 5:24–34).

2. _____ and _____ prayed and praised God through the night after they were beaten and imprisoned for preaching the gospel. God was attracted to their sacrificial worship, and He dispatched an angel to set everyone in the prison free (Acts 16:18–26).

3. A blind man named _____ decided he had nothing to lose, so he displayed his desperation and released such howls of hunger that he overpowered the combined noise of the large crowd that swirled around Jesus. He received his sight and a new life as a result (Mark 10:46–52).

FILLING THE VOID

You are living between "the _____" and "the _____ _____." *It's already promised, but it's not yet delivered.* All you can do is _____ on God—and that is the *best thing to do* when you are living in the _____ of _____, in the in-_____ zone. Welcome to the holy place of _____ emptiness and displayed hunger, one of God's favorite resting places. (p. 95)

NOTES

. . . .

. . . .

. . . .

. . . .

. . . .

. . . .

. . . .

. . . .

. . . .

NOTES

NOTES

7

COLLECTED EMPTINESS

THE VOLUME OF YOUR EMPTINESS DETERMINES THE AMOUNT OF YOUR FILLING

As far as I can tell, hunger is the only thing that has the ability to predetermine how much of God you will receive. How hungry are you? (p. 98)

Why would anyone want to "collect emptiness"? It sounds silly, doesn't it? Yet our daily conversations are peppered with comments linked to emptiness—we just don't use that specific term. How many times have people invited you to their home for a meal with the added phrase, "And make sure you bring your appetite . . . you'll need it." Simply insert the word *emptiness* for appetite and you will understand my point.

The only time people *collect emptiness* is when they anticipate "a filling" with something far more valuable than what they already have in their containers. Is there a better reason to *collect emptiness* than to receive *God's fullness* in return?

Erroneous Assumptions, Presumptions, and Misaligned Paradigms

I don't mean to hurt anyone's feelings, but it appears that the real harbinger of revival is not a good preacher or a good singer—it is the amount of our "collected hunger."

The "God of More Than Enough" is inexorably drawn to the empty capacity of our growling spiritual stomachs, especially when we gather in one mind and one accord with an unappeasable appetite for Him. (p. 98)

Human beings like clear cause-and-effect relationships. If revival ignites somewhere, we assume that "something" triggered it—something we can duplicate that will benefit us. We really hope that "something" allows us to enjoy the benefits without taking any of the responsibility. Perhaps you've noticed that God doesn't work that way.

Our responsibility for *hunger* is unavoidable on the individual and corporate levels. You and I are *called* to hunger for God.

1. What are you hungry for?

2. What do you hunger for in your local church?

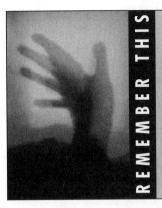

The desperate widow and mother had no idea that the volume of her collected emptiness was going to determine her future. She didn't know how it would all work out; all she knew was to obey God's command. She didn't realize that her cumulative emptiness would literally determine the measure of her miraculous filling. (p. 99)

What Do You Think?

Some of us are determined to "present our fullness for God to fill." Then we complain to anyone who will listen that this "intimacy with God stuff" is a hoax. God isn't interested in meeting you at your best—*that is really when you are at your worst.* He isn't interested in blessing your independence; He responds to your dependence. His strength is attracted to your weakness. He casts down the proud, but He runs to the pitiful. (p. 100)

1. What do you think? Do we instinctively approach our heavenly Father in the same way we approached our earthly parents, proudly displaying our accomplishments in hopes of praise?

2. What do you think? Have you ever wanted to display your disappointment by telling someone, "This 'intimacy with God stuff' is a hoax"? Are you comfortable offering God your brokenness and dependence?

TAKE IT PERSONALLY!

God says, "Pour out whatever oil you have. Empty yourself so I can fill you with more of Myself." *The volume of your emptiness determines the amount of your filling. He can't fill anything more than what you present to Him.* (p. 101)

More Erroneous Assumptions, Presumptions, and Misaligned Paradigms

Our problem is our diet. We like to stuff ourselves on spiritual junk food and feast on dainty bless-me treats. That is the kind of spiritual "food" that has all the form and outward appearance of godliness, but is a standing denial of its power. When the real meat and bread of His presence is placed in front of us, we turn away from His table of intimacy to look for another "quick and easy" flesh-blessing snack at the shallow-food bar. The unpleasant truth is that God is under no obligation to feed casual nibblers at His Communion table. (p. 101)

"Casual nibbling" is the trademark of someone who isn't hungry for some reason or another. We assume that God's grace obligates Him to feed everyone at His table. He does lay food on the table for all who would eat, but He does not prepare smorgasbord fare loaded with sweet but worthless delicacies for every finicky eater. Please mark true or false after each of the statements concerning this passage from *The God Catchers*:

1. Casual nibblers tend to be drawn to the sweet "bless-me" treats, the personal benefits and emotional thrills of flirtation with divinity. True or false?

2. Casual nibbling allows us to lightly taste God's fare without making any commitment to complete the course and accept its obligations. True or false?

3. Casual nibblers who have filled up with dainty bless-me treats instead of life-changing "bread of His presence" will have no strength to stand in times of trial and adversity. True or false?

4. If the Scriptures are right, then the "real meat and bread of His presence" from His table of intimacy produces joy and strength in those who draw near (Neh. 8:10; Ps. 16:11). True or false?

What Do You Think?

People who aren't really hungry, especially those who enter His presence fresh from the bless-me church smorgasbord, tend to sample a little here and snack a little there with extended pinkies in mock discernment. They appear to be looking for "just the right feeling" or "just the right song" to get in the mood for communion with God.

God is looking for really hungry people. He hopes to find them in the church, but if necessary He will bypass an entire temple filled with dainty casual nibblers just to find a few really hungry people on the street, in a bar, or on the wrong side of town. (p. 102)

1. What do you think? How would you classify yourself: as a casual feeder or a starved gorger?

2. What do you think? Are there examples in the Bible where God bypassed the religiously complacent to fellowship with the uncommonly hungry? (See Matt. 9:10–13; Luke 15:1–10.)

REMEMBER THIS

Really hungry people tend to be really desperate people. In the natural, true hunger can turn an honest man into a dishonest man, and it can transform a nonviolent man into a violent maniac. True hunger will make you do things you never, ever thought you would do (in the natural and in the spiritual realm). (p. 102)

Remember Where You've Been, But Always Dare to Dream

Do you remember the first time you saw His face, the first time that you had an encounter with His presence? If you do, then you understand why people will put up with three weeks of bad church for just thirty seconds of His presence. They just keep coming in the fervent hope that somewhere, someday, man will get out of the way so they can see Him. The first time you see His face hooks you for eternity. (pp. 103–4)

1. Describe your first encounter with God.

2. Do you know what it is like to "put up with three weeks of bad church for just thirty seconds of His presence"? If so, then describe your dream for the local church you attend.

FILLING THE VOID

Some of us need to _____ about the _____ of others around us and put our _____ on _____. Daddy is saying to us, "If you want a plastic _____ or spiritual _____, you can have it. If you are _____ _____, I have an infinite supply of My _____ for your unquenchable _____." We need to drop our _____ _____ and stop pretending we are full, well, and blessed. The truth is that we are _____, _____, and desperate for ____. (p. 103)

What Do You Think?

When you collect emptiness or create emptiness by sowing "what you have" into the promises of God, you are living between "the already promised" and the "not yet delivered." You are banking on the faithfulness and compassion of God, who always responds to human emptiness with divine fullness. (p. 104)

1. What do you think? Have you been collecting and sowing emptiness? Do you know what I mean by living between "the already promised" and the "not yet delivered"? Explain.

2. What do you think? Why should anyone want to bank on God? (After all, you can't even see Him.)

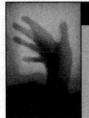

REMEMBER THIS

God wants to break outside our centuries-old religious box. That means our hunger has to get bigger than the box. (p. 105)

More Erroneous Assumptions, Presumptions, and Misaligned Paradigms

Sometimes it seems that we have no idea what hunger does to God . . .

Collected emptiness is one of the keys to citywide and nationwide revival because our collected and collective hunger may even cause God to bend the rules of the universe. Ask Moses! Ask Hezekiah! He has frozen the movements of the cosmos at the sound of a worshipful prayer. He has made the dead to rise and struck down the mighty and proud in response to the fervent cry of emptiness and hunger. (p. 105)

Hunger seems so "nonreligious" that we automatically assume it shouldn't be included in any thinking person's faith portfolio. I'm not sure what should be in a thinking person's faith portfolio, but if hunger isn't in it, then God probably can't be found there either. Thinking, in and of itself, does not draw us closer to God. The Bible uses more passionate terms to describe how God wants us to act toward Him (fill in the missing words from Matt. 22:37–40):

Jesus said to him, "'You shall ____ the LORD your God with ___ your _____, with all your ____, and with all your ____.' This is the first and great commandment. And the second is like it: 'You shall ____ your neighbor as yourself.' On these two commandments ____ ___ the Law and the Prophets."

FILLING THE VOID

We need to present _____ _____ because we need His _____ fullness to bring a _____ of _____ ____ to the desert of human existence. _____ is not a natural process of time; revival occurs only when _____ visits ____. Revival requires _____ _____ and the _____ of natural _____ because you really only have revival when "something that is ____ comes ____ to ____." (p. 106)

What Do You Think?

Part of our problem is that we like to collect all the wrong things for the wrong reasons. We like to collect facts about other people so we can hold their humanness over them like some kind of religious club. We also like to collect facts about God. We don't necessarily *do anything* with the knowledge; we just collect it and hold it up to Him as if it will impress Him. We listen to thousands of hours of teaching and preaching in our lifetimes, but those who know us are sometimes hard-pressed to verify we have anything life-changing to show for it. (p. 106)

What do you think about these statements?

TAKE IT
PERSONALLY!

Our churches are filled with people who could win Bible trivia contests because they are diligent fact collectors where God is concerned. Unfortunately too few of them know the difference between knowing *about* God and *knowing God.*

. . . Sometimes our compulsive collection of secondhand facts about God can create a false sense of intimacy with deity. (pp. 106–7)

More Erroneous Assumptions, Presumptions, and Misaligned Paradigms

Our written source of information about God is admittedly absolutely accurate and certified, but God never intended for us to seek knowledge of His Word apart from seeking Him personally. One should always point to the other. Otherwise we are "always learning and never able to come to the knowledge of the truth." (p. 107)

There are two "ditches" we must avoid at all costs: the ditch of personal experience with no regard or knowledge of God's Word; and the ditch of all head knowledge from the Word of God with no personal experience with the God of the Word. Both ditches lead to a dangerous end. What does God's Word say about it?

Explain how each of the following Scripture passages applies to this discussion:

1. "All Scripture is given by inspiration of God, and is profitable for doctrine, for reproof, for correction, for instruction in righteousness, that the man of God may be complete, thoroughly equipped for every good work" (2 Tim. 3:16–17).

2. "Be doers of the word, and not hearers only, deceiving yourselves" (James 1:22).

3. "The hour is coming, and now is, when the true worshipers will worship the Father in spirit and truth; for the Father is seeking such to worship Him" (John 4:23).

REMEMBER THIS

The spiritual atmosphere of a city is disrupted when people come to church pursuing His presence. (p. 107)

More Erroneous Assumptions, Presumptions, and Misaligned Paradigms

I confess to you that if there is a secret that I could leave with you in this book, it is this: your hunger will take you to places in God that nothing else can. Hunger for Him can take you higher and move His presence closer to you than you ever dreamed. By God's design, He is moved and attracted by the hunger of the human heart.

A nursing mom could more easily say no to her hungry baby than God could say no to a hungry heart. (p. 108)

Many Christians would associate an easy chair or a bolted-down and heavily padded pew, not a journey, with Christianity. This reflects their assumption that the Christian faith doesn't require movement. A brief survey of one of the verbs Jesus used in His statements to the disciples makes the point (fill in the key word):

1. Then He said to them, "_____ Me, and I will make you fishers of men" (Matt. 4:19).

2. Then Jesus said to His disciples, "If anyone desires to come after Me, let him deny himself, and take up his cross, and _____ Me" (Matt. 16:24).

3. Jesus said, "If anyone serves Me, let him _____ Me; and where I am, there My servant will be also. If anyone serves Me, him My Father will honor" (John 12:26).

TAKE IT
PERSONALLY!

The attraction that allows you to "catch" God has nothing to do with how well you have done or how good you think you have been. It has more to do with how hungry you are. God's senses are dull to the supposed strengths and virtues of mankind, but He takes notice at the slightest hint of divine desperation and holy hunger in the least of us. (p. 109)

What Do You Think?

For too long the church has trumpeted to the nations, "He's here! He's here!" when there wasn't enough of Him there to make the church discernibly different from the world. Our claims were true in the sense that the omnipresent God was present in our churches, but that is no claim to fame. His omnipresence is everywhere, even in bars and nightclubs. It's His manifest presence that we must become hungry for, those undeniable moments when you know . . . *He's here!* (p. 109)

What do you think? Is there enough of Him in your life or in your church to make you different from the world? Why or why not?

REMEMBER THIS

God has enough glory to flood the earth to overflowing. The problem isn't whether or not God is enough. The only things that determine how much oil of His presence flows among us are how empty we are and how much unity we can collect. (p. 111)

NOTES

....

....

....

....

....

....

....

....

....

....

NOTES

NOTES

8

How to Carry Hot Coffee

RETAINING THE FRESH DEPOSIT OF GOD

*The only way we can properly carry the full measure of
"God's hot coffee" is to release or relinquish everything that He
hasn't put in our hands in the first place. (p. 125)*

The very idea of my daughter's first attempt to carry hot coffee still makes me nervous years after the fact, but experience told me beforehand that the adventure was inevitable. All of my daughters grew up knowing their daddy was a coffee drinker. They saw me smile almost every time someone successfully delivered a cup of hot java to me without spilling it, so it was only natural for them to want to get into the act.

God expects every serious God Chaser to take the inevitable step of faith to become a *carrier of the divine deposit*. It isn't easy, especially that first attempt, but it is inevitable for everyone who is serious about pleasing the

Father and doing His will on earth. I've been working at it for a little while, but I'm still eager to do anything I can to successfully carry God's cup without spilling it. I want to see Him smile upon me once again.

What Do You Think?

Have you ever experienced something that was so wonderful, extraordinary, and delightful that you never wanted it to end? . . .

God also creates new moments we never want to end when He walks into the middle of our worship service, prayer meeting, or personal devotional time and reveals a glimpse of His glory. How do you retain something so wonderful and so fleeting? (p. 114)

1. What do you think? Have you experienced an extraordinary encounter with God that you never wanted to end? Describe it.

2. How do you hold on to such moments?

TAKE IT
PERSONALLY!

How do you carry the fresh encounter of God in your inward vessel? *How does a church body guard the divine deposit from one worship experience to the next?* How do you "take this home" in real life?

Walk carefully and be aware of His every movement in your heart . . . When He invades your empty space of hunger, turn to meet Him in your spirit. Answer His gentle summons as the young man named Samuel did. (pp. 115–16)

FILLING THE VOID

Prepare a place of _____, _____, _____, and _____ for Him, and invite Him to turn aside and dwell with you. "What do ____ want, Lord? How can we _____ and _____ You tonight, Lord?"

This is how you run your fingers along the pleats of the veil between the _____ and _____ realms. Suddenly your spirit finds a window, a crack leading _____ the bounds of _____, _____, and _____. The sweet fragrance of the Father's _____ _____ will billow through as He comes close to _____ ___ the _____ of your sacrifice of _____. "It's You, Lord! We knew You would come again." (p. 116)

What Do You Think?

If you are talking to your friends and you suddenly feel a wave of His presence roll over you, just stop talking and see what He wants. I stop preaching when I feel a wave of His presence, no matter how many people are watching me. That is the time to silently pray, *Do You want anything? God, You are in charge.*

Learn to carry His presence so you can become a contagious carrier. (p. 117)

1. What do you think? Has this ever happened to you? Describe it.

2. How did you handle the situation then? What would you do differently now?

REMEMBER THIS

The truth is that the presence of God comes on the shoulders of men and women, and it always has. A program will never usher the presence of God into a church. (pp. 117–18)

Erroneous Assumptions, Presumptions, and Misaligned Paradigms

All biblical worship, especially in the Old Testament, was characterized by a *sacrifice*. In the eons of human existence before the Son of God invaded our world and shed His blood to purchase our freedom, only animal blood could permit men to draw near God's presence. Now we can draw near to Him through the blood of Christ and offer Him the sacrifice of praise and present our bodies as living sacrifices. God provided for us, but our obligation to present something to Him is as binding as it ever was. (p. 118)

Most of us *presume* that all sacrifices ended the day Jesus offered Himself on the cross to atone for our sins. It is true that we no longer offer animal sacrifices for sin or forgiveness; but it is not true that God no longer delights in any sacrifices! According to the Old and New Testaments, God is still very interested in certain types of sacrifice.

1. The apostle Paul told us that God expects us to offer this kind of sacrifice, even after Jesus completed His work on the cross (Rom. 12:1).

2. John the revelator described another ancient sacrifice that is offered to God at the end of time (Rev. 8:3–4).

3. This eternal sacrifice has blessed God on "both sides" of the Cross (Ps. 54:6; Heb. 13:15).

4. Jesus told the Samaritan woman that the Father personally seeks people to offer this sacrifice to Him (John 4:23–24).

FILLING THE VOID

The only way God's _____ will _____ over an entire city and region is if His people learn how to _____ His _____ in their undying _____ for Him and _____ it with them. This kind of _____ _____ so brightly that it gives __ _____ to "respect of persons" or _____ _____. Labels and religious _____ fall away and lose their power in its _____. The only thing _____ will recognize is the _____ of its _____. (p. 119)

What Do You Think?

What would happen if the glory of God broke over your entire city or region? Think of the far-reaching effects it would have on the people who live there.

Are you willing to stand in the gap until God breaks out over your city? (p. 119)

1. What do you think? Imagine what would happen in your town or city, and describe it.

2. Are you willing? What do you think it will take to see God break out over your city?

TAKE IT PERSONALLY!

Some people automatically assume that "this God Chaser stuff" is all about the selfish pursuit of just another "religious buzz." No, it is all about God and His purposes, not about us. (p. 119)

More Erroneous Assumptions, Presumptions, and Misaligned Paradigms

God may allow us to "catch" Him, but He will never allow us to leave His presence unchanged. His glory has a way of changing and transforming mortals. Somehow we come away from these encounters more attuned to His loving compassion for the lost and hurting around us. Rather than drive us inward, His manifest presence always turns our eyes away from ourselves and toward others. It drives us beyond the four walls of our meeting halls to seek and save the lost. (p. 120)

People who have never experienced a genuine encounter with God's manifest presence may be tempted to dismiss accounts of God Chasers who became God Catchers as useless tales invented by emotional experience seekers. The assumption is that God Chasers are so obsessed with their quest for emotionalism that they totally abandon their obligation to spread the gospel and serve the needs of others.

1. Have you ever experienced the manifest presence of God? Did it leave you unchanged or forever hungry for another encounter with Him?

2. Did your encounter with divinity cause you to abandon hurting and lost humanity?

3. It has been my experience that God *imparts His heart* for the lost in genuine encounters with hungry believers. How about you?

Remember Where You've Been, But Always Dare to Dream

Unfortunately God's visitation rarely turns into habitation because of our human tendency to immediately turn our focus away from His face to concentrate on the "good feelings" His presence creates in our bodies and souls. These side benefits are wonderful, but we must keep our central focus on God, not on the pleasant side effects of His presence. (p. 120)

Have you ever turned your focus away from God and toward the feelings and exhilaration you felt in His presence? What happened, and how would you do things differently?

What Do You Think?

Anytime God visits you with a miracle, an outpouring of His Spirit, or the beginnings of true revival, the enemy will come and attempt to steal the promise and destroy the deposit the Lord gave you. A woman in Elisha the prophet's day discovered this unpleasant pattern, but her careful preparation met the enemy's attack head-on. The key is that she made room for God's presence in advance. Her example offers clues for your own preparations for the habitation of God and the enemy's attempt to kill or steal His divine deposit. (p. 121)

1. What do you think? Has this ever happened to you? Describe it.

2. How would you "make room for God's presence" in advance?

REMEMBER THIS

Would you consider remodeling your house to accommodate God? Why not? He "remodeled" His house by tearing down the middle wall of separation to accommodate you and me! You must make room for Him if you want visitation to turn into habitation. (p. 122)

More Erroneous Assumptions, Presumptions, and Misaligned Paradigms

Has your divine promise from God dropped dead in the field of dreams? Is your hope for a miracle lingering between a comatose state and a grave of adverse circumstances? Have you watched the children God gave you slip away into sin, rebellion, or bad company while your heart broke for the hundredth time?

It is time to lay the broken, fallen, and dying things in your life on the bed of worship in the room of praise that you prepared for Him. *It isn't over until God says it is over . . .*

Do you have a place of visitation where you can rest your dead or dying visions and hopes? Begin to prepare for His habitation now, even before He shows up. You have to create the empty space and furnish it with your hunger, your worship, and your praise. (pp. 123–24)

1. What do you think? Can you personally relate to the woman of Shunem? Is something or someone near and dear to you in danger or near death because of the enemy's attack? What does this passage say to your heart?

2. Do you have a "place of visitation" in your life? What are you willing to do to prepare for His habitation?

TAKE IT
PERSONALLY!

Part of "carrying" the glory means being willing to release other things we may think are necessary . . . He expects us to put *both hands to the plow* or not even make the attempt. (pp. 124–25)

FILLING THE VOID

We must be willing to _____ and relinquish _____ in all its forms if we want God's _____ _____ to remain among us. Some of us need a _____ of God to release our _____ on our _____ and our brethren. So be it. The alternative is to follow the path of the _____ and _____ who gathered together every _____ to worship and revere an _____ _____ while turning their backs on the _____ of the Sabbath. Who wants to _____ ___ _____ by worshiping the _____-made _____ of _____ and _____ in the name of "stability"? (p. 126)

What Do You Think?

Every organized church body has its own strengths and weaknesses, and each of us must fight individual battles with our desire for comfort and the stability of predictability versus our hunger for the presence of the eternal God.

You are reading this book because there is something in you that is determined to pursue Him at any cost. If you have "caught" Him even once in your life, then you will do almost anything to catch Him again. (p. 127)

1. What do you think? Are there visible weaknesses in your life or in your local church body or denomination that can potentially obstruct your passionate pursuit of God? Describe them.

2. What put you in the chase for God's manifest presence? Have you ever "caught" Him? How desperate are you to encounter His presence again?

REMEMBER THIS

As difficult as it sounds, the possibilities are endless: "If God could ever find . . . people in a church—who will band together, the amount of power He would release to them to dispel demonic powers would be in direct proportion to the amount of unity they achieve." (p. 126)

A Prayer for Passion

We are passionate for one thing—You. Set our hearts on fire with hunger; make us miserably desperate for more of You. Set Your hot coal of hunger and holiness on our tongues and in our hearts. We long for You.

Let Your fire burn in our churches; let the fire blaze in our homes. It's not a man that we want; we want You, Lord. Show us Your face, God. (p. 128)

NOTES

. . . .

. . . .

. . . .

. . . .

. . . .

. . . .

. . . .

. . . .

. . . .

. . . .

NOTES

THE SECRET OF
THE STAIRS

O my dove, that art in the clefts of the rock,

in the secret places of the stairs, let me see thy countenance,

let me hear thy voice; for sweet is thy voice, and thy countenance is comely.[1]

As human beings, we exert a large percentage of our energy in search of romance during our early adult years. After we find a mate, we expend even more energy (or should) preserving our romantic relationships. One of the mysteries of romance that makes it so intriguing is the concept of "privileged access."

When you find someone who mysteriously moves from the status of acquaintance and friend to the exclusive position of your "beloved," you automatically extend to that person certain privileges withheld from all others.

Your beloved has *privileged access* to your most intimate emotions, your dreams, and ultimately, even to your weaknesses. In extreme circumstances, lovers may even extend the privileged access of life itself by laying down their lives to save their beloved ones. If you wonder about the source of the mystery of privileged access, ask yourself, "In whose image were we made?"

Erroneous Assumptions, Presumptions, and Misaligned Paradigms

One time I took [my wife] to visit a man who, according to my mother, actually taught me how to walk during my infancy. When I knocked on the front door, it was obvious that he and his wife weren't home. My wife turned around to go back to the car, and I said, "Where are you going?" She said, "They're not home, so I'm going back to the car." (p. 130)

Have you ever "gone back to the car" because you thought God "wasn't home" after you knocked at the front door with a few songs, an opening prayer, and a sermon? Explain.

What Do You Think?

I explained to my bride, "It is understood in this area that if some folks tell you where they have hidden the key to their house, then they won't mind you making coffee in their kitchen." When someone shows you his hidden key, he has given you family privileges.

God has shown us His hidden key—the key to His heart and the secret place of access to divine intimacy. (p. 131)

1. What do you think? Knowing that God has given you the hidden key to His heart and His presence, how do you intend to use it?

2. Is it presumptuous to think you have been given the right to approach God's throne, or is it presumptuous to think you have not? (Hint: See Eph. 2:17–19; Heb. 10:19–22.)

FILLING THE VOID

Unfortunately centuries of ___ _____ _____ and our _____ to the stuff of _____ muddied the waters of our _____ _____ relationship with divinity. We have used ___-_____, religion-based _____ and methods to rebuild the _____ that _____ God and man—after Jesus _____ His _____ _____ to break them down. (p. 131)

More Erroneous Assumptions, Presumptions, and Misaligned Paradigms

It is true that even at our best we are rather pitiful, but that is why we are saved by grace and not by works. It is also true that God is holy, mighty, all-powerful, all-knowing, and present everywhere. However, the word *aloof* simply does not apply to the God who came down to sacrifice His own Son on a Roman cross to restore His fellowship with our fallen race. (pp. 131–32)

The human habit of expanding or omitting crucial details of the truth can create tremendous problems at times. When we describe events, we tend to remember what we understand and omit or reconstruct what we can't comprehend or appreciate. Omitted or fabricated details can produce dangerous paradigms in the realm of faith. One of the most dangerous paradigms afflicting the church is the idea that God is aloof from us. Check the possible sources of the "aloof God" concept:

❑ "Well, all I know is that He didn't answer my prayer, even though I said everything right and used Jesus' name at the end."

❑ "I think God plays favorites. He talks only with people who have TV shows."

❑ "I've gone to church all of my life, and I've never felt Him there. Doesn't that qualify as aloof?"

❑ "Didn't God live in darkness inside a private room behind a veil? Doesn't the Bible say no man can ever see Him?"

(Author's note: I deal with each of these statements in *The God Catchers* and *The God Chasers*.)

What Do You Think?

Some newer church traditions seem to throw out any idea that God is holy, supremely just, and all-powerful. By the time modern man was finished with Him, He was barely God at all . . . As a result, many people take God's grace for granted, almost as if they *deserve* His grace. How can that make sense? *If it is deserved, it isn't grace. If it is grace, then it isn't deserved.* (p. 132)

1. What do you think? Does this seem like the ditch opposite from the "aloof God" ditch? Explain.

2. God isn't aloof from us, but our sin does separate us from Him. Grace is His answer, and through Jesus, we are drawn near to Him. Can you explain the problem we create when we begin to think we actually earned grace or somehow deserve it? (Hint: Think like a spoiled child who believes she earned or deserves all of the gifts she receives at a birthday party or at Christmas.)

REMEMBER THIS

We must seek His face, not just His hands. Bless the Blesser, and the blessings of His hands will come naturally. (p. 133)

More Erroneous Assumptions, Presumptions, and Misaligned Paradigms

We also have a dangerous tendency to celebrate the men and women God has blessed more than the God who blessed them. In some cases, the celebration becomes so extravagant that it borders on "the idolatry of the anointed." Perhaps we should remind people in our meetings, "Remember that you didn't come to see me; you came to see Him. You don't need the hand of man laid on your head as much as you need the presence of God to touch your heart." (p. 133)

A misaligned paradigm is a crooked way of thinking and logic disconnected from the truth and waiting to collapse in a harmful way. When we idolize the anointed servants of God rather than give all honor to God, we are like the death row inmate who kisses and praises the prison warden who delivers the notice of pardon.

1. The inmate had (*a*) nothing or (*b*) everything to do with the pardon.

2. The fellow inmate (*a*) authorized the release by his own authority or (*b*) merely delivered a message from a higher authority outside and higher than the correctional institution.

3. The only one who deserves the kiss and all of the praise is (*a*) the inmate carrying the message or (*b*) the governor who authorized and signed the decree of pardon.

4. Perhaps ministers of the gospel should say, (*a*) "Thank you, I do the best I can," or (*b*) "Don't praise or worship me; I'm just delivering the good news and gifts from the King of glory. Come out of your 'cell' and meet Him face-to-face. Give Him all of the praise."

(Answer key: 1-a, 2-b, 3-b, 4-b)

TAKE IT PERSONALLY!

I believe in the biblical practice of "the laying on of hands," but I have discovered that *His touch* is always preferred over the God-anointed touch of man. Both are good, but His touch is far better. (p. 133)

FILLING THE VOID

We "_____" the prophets who can tell us the _____ of ____'s hearts, but where are the prophets who can tell us the _____ of ____'s heart? We plan our _____, _____ our sermons, and _____ our songs to _____ ____, but where is the _____ that knows how to move the _____ of ____? (p. 133)

More Erroneous Assumptions, Presumptions, and Misaligned Paradigms

God wants to raise up a generation of God-pleasers, not the run-of-the-mill religious man-pleasers. Our destiny is founded upon His wisdom and purposes, not the ever-changing whims and wishes of men. That means the church desperately needs people who possess "the secret of the stairs" Solomon alluded to in his Song of Songs . . .

. . . this phrase that clearly conveys the privileged access of the lover to the Beloved. This is the path of exclusive passion, of worship reserved only for God. This is the *secret of the stairs,* the portal of privileged access enjoyed only by true worshipers. (p. 134)

At times it seems as if we've built our church structure on the bedrock of "run-of-the-mill religious man-pleasers." It has become "the monolith of the mediocre," "the luxury palace of the complacently lukewarm majority."

1. In your opinion, is there any truth to the terms used here to describe the modern church? Explain.

2. What word or words describe those possessing "the secret of the stairs" that could never be applied to those who are happily lounging in "the monolith of the mediocre" or are dozing in "the luxury palace of the complacently lukewarm majority"?

3. Is it ridiculous or eternally right to believe we should pursue God with passion and hunger? Explain in your own words.

What Do You Think?

Explain to me why God singled out five men in the Old Testament the way He did. In the book of Ezekiel, God said, *"Even if these three men, Noah, Daniel, and Job, were in it,* they would deliver only themselves by their righteousness." God also declared in the book of Jeremiah: *"Even if Moses and Samuel stood before Me,* My mind would not be favorable toward this people . . ."

These men managed to get close enough to God to win His heart in some way. This is the power of proximity personified. We are not talking about bribery or flattery; we are talking about God Chasers who knew how to pursue Him with genuine passion in ways that drew Him close. Noah, Daniel, Job, Moses, and Samuel—they all drew close to God in spite of impossible crises and adverse circumstances. (pp. 134–35)

1. What do you think? Were the accomplishments of these men isolated events confined exclusively to the ancient era? Is the "power of proximity" off-limits to you? Explain.

2. What can you do that these men did in their day?

FILLING THE VOID

Noah continued to _____ ___ in obedience despite _____ _____ of his ___ project. He endured the taunts, laughter, and _____ _____ _____ of neighbors while he constructed a _____ in a place with virtually no _____ and absolutely no _____! It was the equivalent of building an _____ _____ in your _____ in the middle of the _____ _____, yet Noah did it and _____ God with his _____ of _____ through obedience. In the end, Noah's righteousness and humility before God _____ his entire _____ and the _____ ____ as well. (pp. 135–36)

More Erroneous Assumptions, Presumptions, and Misaligned Paradigms

[Daniel] consistently put God first above the approval of men and even above his own safety and comfort. He also realized that his privileged access to God was meant to benefit more than just himself. He had a responsibility to stand in the gap for others, exactly as another higher and greater Intercessor would one day stand in the gap of sin for the human race. (p. 137)

All of us occasionally battle the problem of selfishness and self-centered perspective. This is especially noticeable when we receive blessings or special abilities from God. At first, most people are careful to remain humble and give God the glory. Over time, however, we tend to change our paradigm and forget why the Giver gave us the gifts in the first place.

If you examine Daniel's life, you realize that (*choose one or more correct answers*)

1. as a God Chaser (and by faith, as a God Catcher), you have been given your power of proximity to God's presence for (*a*) all of the good feelings it gives you, (*b*) God's pleasure and blessing, (*c*) intercession, so you can stand in the gap for others, (*d*) love's sake, as the Father blesses the children He loves.

2. the pursuit of God is (*a*) something you can do as convenience allows, (*b*) a lifestyle, a continuous process of diligent search and joyful discovery, (*c*) vital to the fulfillment of divine purpose and personal destiny, (*d*) totally dependent on your ability to put God first in all things.

(Answer key: 1-b, c, d; 2-b, c, d)

REMEMBER THIS

[Job] became God's "poster child for God Chasers" when he proved under extreme hardship that his love was directed to the Giver of blessings, not the blessings of the Giver. (p. 137)

FILLING THE VOID

Perhaps Moses' _____ _____ of _____ to the Father is revealed in this one-of-a-kind conversation with God: "So the _____ said to Moses, 'I will also __ _____ _____ that you have spoken; *for you have _____ _____ in My sight, and I ____ you by ____.'* And he said, 'Please, _____ me ____ _____.'"

As I wrote in *The God Chasers*, "This _____ _____ to see God's _____, to see Him ____ to ____, is one of the most important ____ to _____, _____, and the fulfillment of ___'s _____ on the earth." (p. 139)

What Do You Think?

[Samuel] learned to hear God's still small voice as a young boy in the temple. He never forgot how to listen to and serve divinity. His relationship with God was so unique in that spiritually dry era that the Scriptures say, "So Samuel grew, and the LORD was with him and *let none of his words fall to the ground.*" How many of us can make that claim today? This God Catcher knew how to touch the heart of God and change his world. (p. 139)

1. What do you think? Is it unrealistic to dream of honing your spiritual listening and answering skills so much that, as He did with Samuel, God would "let none of your words fall to the ground"?

2. Is something about this impossible dream stirring your heart? What will you sacrifice to pursue God so diligently that He goes with you and guards your words? How can you touch the heart of God and change your world?

More Erroneous Assumptions, Presumptions, and Misaligned Paradigms

The five men seemingly hand selected by God in the Old Testament era seemed to know about and understand what Solomon called "the secret of the stairs." These men knew this secret "back stairs" access to God's presence can produce a celestial "yes" when every earthly circumstance says "no." Passionate worship will weave its way through the trappings of failure, discouragement, and difficulty to bring you to the place of passion with Him. (p. 140)

You and I live in a finite, material world largely ruled by circumstances. Although the church is actually a supernatural institution founded upon divine foundations, its members still live and operate as if "circumstances" are the final authority in life. Answer these questions to the best of your ability:

1. You are a pastor, and you sense that God wants your local church congregation to plant a church in a nearby inner-city neighborhood. In response, you should

   a. submit God's request to the board of elders or deacons for their final decision of approval or rejection.

    b. count the cost and immediately dismiss it if the project cost exceeds cash on hand or available human and material resources.

    c. put God's assignment to a congregational vote.

    d. pray, pursue Him, and seek the proper way to share the vision with other leaders in the church and with the local body. Then follow through with His communication instructions while firmly informing all those involved that you know you have heard from God, and that you will obey, even if you must do it out of your own resources.

2. You are a faithful churchgoer with a deep hunger for more of God. Now you hear a rumor that God is seeking passionate worshipers at a cost:

    a. You squelch those rumors and faithfully report the names of the troublemakers to your church cult committee.

    b. You ask everyone you know if he has seen Him. Are the rumors true?

    c. You risk everything to seize the day and pursue the prize of the upward calling to His presence.

    d. Instead of resisting your heart's impulse to cast caution to the wind, you yield to it—only to find that your passion increases and your desperation for Him get out of hand.

    e. You devote your life to pursuing His presence, stringing together divine encounters with Him like a string of precious pearls.

(Answer key: You will find the answers in the inner chambers of your heart, and the Word and Spirit of God will confirm them.)

TAKE IT
PERSONALLY!

You are after *more* than the blessings of His hands; you want the glory of His face. You've made up your mind and refined your pursuit to the point where you no longer seek a blessing; you are after nothing less than the Blesser. (p. 141)

FILLING THE VOID

Someday you will be _____ the _____ for things that _____ says are _____: "That can't be _____. There is ___ ____ that can be taken care of. Don't you know ____ ____ __ ____, and that _____ is ___ of the _____?" At the same time, _____ is saying, "I think I know a way. There is a _____ _____, a _____ _____ that can lead you there, but the _____ ___ to reach it is through _____ _____." (p. 143)

What Do You Think?

The second level of encounter in our journey of pursuit is the "secret place of the stairs," where we pursue Him passionately as His bride, using every means at our disposal. He gives us the secret place of access through passionate worship, but we must supply the passion and the active pursuit. (p. 144)

1. What do you think? Is this what you were taught as a little child? Why not?

2. God pursued us in His "passion," carrying a bloodied cross through the streets of the Holy City while His blood flowed from a forehead crowned with thorns. It seems to me that all of us should be taught about passion in childhood. If we must choose between passion for God or stability for humanity, which would you choose and why?

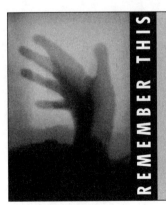

REMEMBER THIS

The first line of divine encounters takes place through the wonderful pursuit of His face, when we chase Him as little children and He allows us to catch Him for a grand reunion of joy and delight . . . we never "graduate" from this level of encounter. (p. 143)

NOTES

NOTES

IO

I Want You, Daddy!

THE CRY GOD CAN'T DENY

Some of God's kids have tripped over a ravel in the carpet of
time while pursuing an encounter with Daddy. There is no need
to explain the niceties of my points to these people; their faces are
already buried in their arms and the carpet is soaked with their tears.
The more of Him they get, the more of Him they want. (p. 160)

It could be argued that this chapter in *The God Catchers* is unnecessary because virtually everyone believes that God answers our prayers of desperation. Even people who barely concede the existence of God have no problem crying out to Him in desperation when trouble comes their way.

The problem isn't that people don't know how to pray desperate prayers in times of need. It is the game playing and pretense that get us. It is humiliating and humbling for us to display desperation, so we cover it up with every disguise we can find.

People who find themselves rushing toward a concrete wall in a careening car will shamelessly scream toward heaven, "My God, help me! Save me!" Should God answer their cry and steer the car clear of the danger, the same people will look around sheepishly and quickly wipe away the tears to avoid revealing the depth of their momentary desperation. I just want to ask them, Why?

Good churchgoers do everything they can to avoid revealing their inner pain and hunger. Yet on the day they find their lives speeding toward destruction through financial collapse, divorce, sickness, or loss, they will scream out shamelessly from the pew or the altar, "My God, help me! Save me!" It is time to drop the game playing and pretense and cry out to Him without shame, for He is quick to answer.

Erroneous Assumptions, Presumptions, and Misaligned Paradigms

Verbal eloquence is no match for the simple passion of a baby's cry, or the passionate plea of a broken and desperate heart . . . Jesus . . . compared the simple passionate prayer of repentance by a lowly tax collector with the empty but eloquent prayer of a proud Pharisee, noting that God heard and answered the sinner while totally ignoring the hypocrite. Eloquence can't be equated with automatic response! (p. 147)

Eagle-eyed spiritual Pharisees, left to their own devices, would quickly whisk away anyone resembling the lowly tax collector. Disturbances of human eloquence are simply not permitted in most churches. God knows. He has tried to gently interrupt our eloquent but empty prayers for multiple generations. He rarely succeeds because we've grown accustomed to the erroneous assumption that soulish eloquence is superior to the passionate but unrehearsed prayer of the spirit. This involves even more erroneous assumptions (*pick them out of the lineup*):

1. God is impressed with our seminary-sharpened intellect. True or false?

2. God prefers carefully framed proclamations that also warm the hearts of human hearers over hoarse and unrehearsed pleas of the passionate and the hungry. True or false?

3. God has no interest in human passion or displayed desperation in church meetings. True or false?

4. In God's view, verbal eloquence is no match for the simple passion of a baby's cry. True or false?

What Do You Think?

I believe there are unused keys of power and divine access lying on the dusty shelves of the church that we have forgotten about. Desperate passion of worship or the painful cries of crisis are going to unlock the heavens for somebody. Most of the time, we just say, "Wonder where those keys are?" It is time for us to perceive and seize the secret keys to the heart of God (and maybe clean out our ecclesiastical junk drawer!). (p. 149)

1. What do you think? If God gave someone the keys long ago, why would he misplace or discard them?

2. What are you going to do now that you've rediscovered some of those keys of privileged access to the heart of God?

REMEMBER THIS

If the determinate length of our waiting actually predetermines the size and passion of His answer, then perhaps that explains why true revival has evaded most of the church. (p. 149)

Remember Where You've Been, But Always Dare to Dream

Sometimes you come in your fullness and make yourself empty like Zacchaeus did. At other times, you cry out in your bankruptcy, hunger, and pain, and God shows up. That's the cry God can't deny. (p. 149)

1. Do you remember times when you "emptied" yourself to reach out for God? What happened?

2. Do you have memories of crying out to God in times of spiritual or physical bankruptcy or desperation? Describe what happened.

FILLING THE VOID

_____ caused God to _____ heaven so He could turn the _____-_____ door of _____ into a secret _____ of _____ to heaven. In His _____ He said, "I have to figure out a way to ____ My _____ in here, even if I have to _____ what was _____." It is _____ that God would _____ His own ____ just to get close to ___, but _____ got in His way. (pp. 151–52)

More Erroneous Assumptions, Presumptions, and Misaligned Paradigms

After centuries of painting passion as something evil and untrustworthy, the church must rediscover the true power of "God-ward passion." I read somewhere that God's Son exhibited His uninhibited passion for His Father's house: "Zeal for Your house has eaten Me up." (p. 152)

Passion is one of those power-packed forces that does great good when released in proper settings, and great evil when released in improper or inappropriate settings. Our problem in the church is that we considered the explosive potential of passion to be too volatile to be released in the church or the life of faith. Consider these examples and decide for yourself:

1. Passion toward your neighbor's spouse is *appropriate* or *inappropriate*.

2. Passion toward your own spouse in the intimacy of marriage is *appropriate* or *inappropriate*.

3. Passion directed toward a political cause, a moral belief, or a sports event is considered by society to be *appropriate* or *inappropriate*.

4. Passion directed toward God and His presence is *appropriate* or *inappropriate*.

REMEMBER THIS

Worship is the process of discovering God's presence. If you want to find Him, you worship your way there most of the time. At times, your journey will be accelerated by passion or by your painful cries in the midst of a crisis. In those times, divinity comes in answer to the *cry God cannot deny.* (pp. 152–53)

What Do You Think?

Perhaps you have gone beyond the stage of casual hunger. You have even surpassed the supercharged arena of hunger fueled by passion. You have reached the point of all-out desperation where you no longer act like yourself. You are *desperate* for an encounter at the face place. Hunger is written all over your face. You have become like Moses who said, in essence, "I'm tired of Your hands; show me Your face, Lord. Show me Your glory." (p. 153)

1. What do you think? Is this an accurate portrait of your spiritual state right now? What are you desperate for?

2. Have you ceased to "act like yourself"? Are you prepared to change forever in His presence when He allows you to catch Him?

I must remind you that you fell in love with God—not His assistants or His gifts. You have reached the point where you can't be satisfied by the arrival of one of God's earthly assistants anymore. Your painful cry is this: "I want *You*, Daddy." (p. 153)

More Erroneous Assumptions, Presumptions, and Misaligned Paradigms

Passionate desperation can turn God Chasers into God Catchers. You can't run fast enough to catch God, but your passionate cry of desperation, your words, can run faster than you can. This isn't an opinion; just ask Hosea the prophet. He said, "Take words with you, and return to the LORD." (p. 154)

Words can become powerless and empty when deprived of either truth or passion. Jesus said the Father is seeking worshipers, but He didn't mention a divine search for theological experts or the evangelical equivalent of Pharisees.

1. Man celebrates the Age of Reason and the romantic period in human history books and philosophy and art courses. It appears that God would rather celebrate the Age of P_____ D_____ and His eternal romance with w_____ers.

2. God isn't impressed with your speed in the one-hundred-yard dash; He is more interested in what you do on your _____ in prayer and worship. He is looking for the kind of _____ _____ that turns God Chasers into God _____.

What Do You Think?

It is time to put a demand on the passion of God. If He ripped the veil of separation in Jerusalem two thousand years ago, then He will rip apart anything that separates you from Him now. He will rip through every obstacle in your life if you put a demand on His passion. You have no idea how much He loves you. Let your worship and hunger cry out to Him in desperation right now. (p. 155)

1. What do you think? Does this statement sound too good to be true? Why?

2. If you doubt whether or not "now" is the time to put a demand on the passion of God, then ask yourself, "When is the right time?" God has been waiting for thousands of years. Why should He wait for you even one day longer?

FILLING THE VOID

One day ____ _____ in various cities around the world will be _____ Him, _____ His face, and _____ for more of His presence, and a tiny pinprick of _____ or _____ _____ will burst the heavens and God's _____ will ____ ____ over the earth. We really won't be able to say it was because of a ___ preaching or a particular _____ singing. It will be because some _____, _____ _____ risked everything to _____ through to give their Master a _____ from the ____ of human _____ and _____ in the House of Bread. (p. 156)

REMEMBER THIS

Do you feel as if you've been pregnant with the promises of God for a long time? You have done everything you know to do to bring it to pass, and now it has brought you to your knees and you are desperate. You have finally arrived in the ultimate posture of worship—*desperate despondency!* (p. 157)

More Erroneous Assumptions, Presumptions, and Misaligned Paradigms

Conventional logic said Saul was doing God a favor by stamping out the heretical followers of the dead Carpenter from Galilee; but in the thirty seconds he spent in the manifest presence of God on the dusty road to Damascus, Saul's heart knowledge leapfrogged past his head knowledge.

He met the resurrected Carpenter from Galilee, and it took three years of isolation in the desert for Paul's theology to catch up with his thirty-second experience with the Messiah in blinding glory. (p. 157)

Conventional logic says the zealous opponents of the passionate pursuit of God in the church are doing God a favor by stamping out wildfire in the body of Christ. These brothers and sisters (*check if correct*)

❏ are sincerely wrong. They simply need to spend thirty seconds in the man-ifest presence of God.

❏ need to drop their wet blankets and just give in to God. They need to be fanning the flames, not trying to put them out.

❏ are still members of Christ's body and must be treated that way.

REMEMBER THIS

If you ever have a genuine heart-sized encounter with Him, then your head will have to say, "I'll have to catch up later." Why? *True passion is illogical, and God's presence ignites passion . . .* Passion is illogical, and passion doesn't put price limits on the cost of the encounter. Passion says, "I don't really care." (pp. 158–59)

What Do You Think?

A woman in labor has gone beyond the definition of hunger and far surpassed the meaning of passion. Now she is openly, unapologetically *desperate* to deliver her gift to the world. So it is with the people of God at the apex of the progression of divine frustration. (p. 159)

1. What do you think? Are you desperate to see the church deliver her gift to the world? Have you gone beyond the definition of hunger?

2. Describe your position on the "progression of divine frustration."

FILLING THE VOID

If you are _____ on a _____ from God, ____ the _____ of your _____ and put it on _____. Make that nagging phone call to heaven and tell Him, "_____, I want ____!"

Forget your _____ so you can have an _____ with His _____. Your _____ can cut through every _____ and _____. Once the Father hears a true ____ of _____ from His children, He _____ to meet them in their _____ with such speed and violence that the "_____ door" of His veiled hiding place is _____ in _____ and left behind. (p. 160)

REMEMBER THIS

Worship is the process where we find Him in our wholeness. Brokenness is the process whereby God finds us in pieces. I am convinced that God hides when we think nothing is wrong, just to preserve the freshness of encounter. (pp. 160–61)

More Erroneous Assumptions, Presumptions, and Misaligned Paradigms

God has no need to "hide" from us in our times of crisis or self-cultivated hunger. When we fall into sin and hurt ourselves or grow desperately frustrated during the pursuit, God immediately shows up. The game is up because the purpose of joy is discovery, not the chase itself.

For the same reason, the Father takes joy in transforming God Chasers into God Catchers. He likes to let you catch Him! The purpose of the pursuit is the finding, not the hiding, and nothing changes the hiding into the finding so quickly as the cry God can't deny. (p. 161)

We tend to do everything we can to look good on the outside, even when we are really dying on the inside. It is the paradigm of the church: look good for God on Sundays, and be yourself the rest of the time. Reverse the statements in the passage cited, and see what truths you discover:

God usually "_____" from us in our times of confidence or ____-confident satisfaction. When we claim to have no ___ and scoff at the idea of desperately p_____ God, then He is careful to ____ from us.

NOTES

NOTES

11

LIVING IN THE VILLAGE OF REPENTANCE AT FRUSTRATION'S ADDRESS

(AND CONTENT TO STAY THERE)

Repentance can accelerate the process of entering His presence. I've often said that repentance "is like worship on steroids." (p. 165)

The concept of living in "the village of frustration" seems at odds with the traditional Christian view of life with the Prince of Peace. A brief look at the life of the apostle Paul should clear up any doubts, however.

God uprooted this man from everything he was taught to be and do. Trained to minister among the most elite and best-educated teachers in ancient Judaism, Paul was retrained—not in a temple but in a desert—and promptly dispatched to minister to non-Jewish people scattered in pagan cities far from Jerusalem. He had every right—and all of the faith necessary—to live a comfortable and outwardly peaceful life as a respected teacher. Instead, he *chose* to live one step behind his Master and one step ahead of imminent martyrdom.

It is one thing to receive salvation through Christ and then sit and wait peacefully for His return. It is another to obey the command of God and become a God Chaser who denies himself, takes up a cross every day, and chases after Him. Paul could have been satisfied with his many accomplishments, but he constantly talked about pressing for more. This is the life of godly frustration marked by continual repentance and sublime discomfort.

What Do You Think?

Once you decide to abandon your permanent place in the pew or leave that comfortable padded seat in the back of the church to chase Him, God issues a permanent change-of-address notice for you. From that moment on, you become a spiritual traveler in transit, a pilgrim on an eternal pilgrimage to the place of His presence. (p. 164)

What do you think? In the note for this statement (on p. 206), I make it clear that being a pilgrim does not include the act of hopping from church to church. What do you think it does mean?

FILLING THE VOID

"But, Tommy, I don't like _____ with this . . . this, this _____ _____. Will I ever stop _____ like I _____ _____ of Him?"

Will it help if I tell you that all the _____ _____ of ages past have _____ at _____ address? Holy _____ is their street in the village of _____, and Divine _____ is their zip code. Their hunger was greater than their _____, and their divine _____ made them _____ _____ like, "Show me Your _____." (p. 164)

Erroneous Assumptions, Presumptions, and Misaligned Paradigms

The full faith of God Himself backs His statement about repentance. It places a legitimate demand on His presence; it fuels it like pressing an accelerator on a car. Our problem is that most of us have a concept of repentance as "an occasional visit to the village of Repentance." God calls us to a lifestyle of repentance, which is living in the village. (p. 165)

1. Are you included in the "most of us"? Do you make only occasional visits to the village of Repentance? Why?

2. Do you believe God has really called us to a lifestyle of repentance? Why?

REMEMBER THIS

God births a frustration in your heart that compels you to pursue Him for *more and more of His presence,* which in turn makes you want Him even more! This is the only true "marriage made in heaven." (p. 166)

What Do You Think?

Our faith isn't based on feelings, but it is *fueled by passion.* We anchor our faith on the things God said and promised in His inspired Word, but passion provides the courage and drive to pursue and serve the God of the Word. (p. 166)

What do you think? Perhaps you were originally taught that passion has nothing to do with faith. What do you think about the relationship between faith and passion now?

More Erroneous Assumptions, Presumptions, and Misaligned Paradigms

We live as if the first commandment says: "Acknowledge the existence of the Lord your God and attend gatherings in respect of His power to send you to hell." It really says, "You shall *love* the LORD your God with *all your heart,* with *all your soul,* and with *all your mind."* Can you find a single laid-back, casual, coolly objective, or calm phrase in that command? (p. 166)

Mentally compare the church "as we know it" with the church "as God says it." How do you and your local church match up to what Jesus confirmed was the first and greatest commandment?

Remember Where You've Been, But Always Dare to Dream

Do you get the feeling something is missing from the typical Sunday morning religious experience we call church? It is God who placed this incredible hunger and divine discontent in you. Even as He blesses you, He ignites a deep hunger and longing in your heart of hearts that cries out, "Daddy, don't send Your assistant . . . I want *You!"* (p. 166)

As you read these words, did you feel that familiar sinking feeling again? Remember that God established the church. Any problems or errors in it can be corrected just as quickly as God can adjust attitudes, change paradigms, and alter our man-centered methods. So remember where you've been, but always dare to dream of moving up from "good" to "best." What are the hungers and longings of your heart?

FILLING THE VOID

He is calling ___ into a _____ and persistent _____ _____ that He characterized as a _____ between a heavenly _____ and His _____, the _____.

Platonic or _____ relationships are a _____ idea; the _____ lifelong _____ of husband and wife was ___ idea. Which one did God choose as a _____ for ___ relationship with the _____? (Which one do we most accurately model in our _____ _____?) (p. 166)

TAKE IT
PERSONALLY!

We are called into a life of dynamic, real-life faith punctuated by alternate waves of nearly unbearable spiritual hunger and the unspeakable joy of His intimate answer to our hunger. I call this state of God-ordained tension "living at frustration's address on Holy Hunger Street in Divine Desperation." (p. 167)

What Do You Think?

It is what you do in those circumstantial moments of divine frustration that determines whether you remain a God Chaser or you become a God Catcher. The first is good, but the second is better; and the truth is that God will constantly move us from the role of chaser to catcher and then to chaser again. After all, we serve a God who moves (and hides). (p. 167)

1. What do you think? Describe some moments of divine frustration in your life, and include a description of what you did.

2. Would you consider yourself a God Chaser? What price are you willing to pay to become a God Catcher as well?

REMEMBER THIS

Pain is pain, but if you can seek Him in the darkness of your midnight, your pain can become the wind beneath your wings that lifts you into His presence! (p. 169)

More Erroneous Assumptions, Presumptions, and Misaligned Paradigms

Pain and brokenness probably brought you to Him in the first place, and pain and brokenness will certainly lead you back to Him without fail. Have you noticed that *the thing God runs to is the very thing we run from?* "He is near to them that are of a broken heart" (and we do everything we can to avoid the pain of brokenness). (p. 170)

Much of the typical church experience is focused on our flight from pain, failure, and death. This is partly due to our God-given sense of survival, but there is something else at work in much of what many Christians do in life.

1. The answer may be found in your response to this question: What role does fear—fear of pain, failure, and death—play in your everyday decisions and relationships?

2. What is God's solution to fear? (See 1 John 4:18.)

FILLING THE VOID

___ _____ are so _____ at times that they make _____ ____ feel frustrated too. It seems that _____ they have is "_____." The _____ God Chasers who become God _____ have a way of entering our meetings with their hair _____ _____ from fresh _____ in an upper room somewhere. They are always looking for another _____ ____ to fan with their _____, so God tends to ____ __ and make it nearly impossible to _____ church __ _____. (p. 171)

What Do You Think?

There are no shortcuts to discipleship. To reach the broken, you must journey through the valley of brokenness yourself and have your "spiritual passport" stamped and verified. Why? The people on your job and in your neighborhood need to see you dealing with the same problems they deal with, but with the joy and strength of the Lord carrying you through while you praise Him. (p. 172)

1. What do you think? Is brokenness really a necessary part of the discipleship process? Why?

2. What impact has your life had on your neighbors, relatives, and coworkers?

The significance of living at frustration's address isn't that we are suffering for more of the Lord; it is that we have learned to worship and praise Him regardless of our circumstances or status in life. (p. 172)

More Erroneous Assumptions, Presumptions, and Misaligned Paradigms

Once we learn how to worship and sing and chase Him even in a dreary midnight hour, we will accomplish more than just having a "sudden visitation" from Him. When God heard the worship rising from that Philippian prison cell, He came so suddenly that His coming triggered an earthquake that shook chains off more than just Paul and Silas. The Bible says that *all* the prisoners were set free. (pp. 172–73)

Instant coffee, instant potatoes, microwave meals, fast-food drive-up windows, and on-line banking—the church has adopted the culture's craving for quick and easy delivery of the things people want most. The only problem is that no one seems to have asked God for His opinion. God does come *suddenly* at times, but it is usually in response to someone who worships Him *stubbornly*.

1. Describe a situation in your life in which you stubbornly worshiped God while believing for His sudden visitation.

2. If you are facing a difficult situation now, what will you do in the middle of it?

TAKE IT PERSONALLY!

Isn't it interesting that the number of prisoners who get set free in your city may depend on whether you can sing through your pain and midnight desperation? It takes us right back to the shocking truth that church is not about you; church is all about Him! (p. 173)

FILLING THE VOID

Something _____ is coming to the _____ residents of _____ _____ Street. The God of ____ ____ _____ is coming in the fullness of time, and some _____ discontented ___ _____ are about to "_____" God by ___ design. Something ____ and _____ is about to _____ and _____ your church, your city, and your home. Can you _____ the _____ required for those who wait on the _____? (p. 175)

What Do You Think?

We need to learn how to leave a worship service hungrier than when we came. If you want to be a God Catcher, you must learn how to live contentedly with divine desperation and holy hunger at frustration's address! (p. 176)

1. What do you think? How is it possible to leave a worship service "hungrier" than when you came?

2. Have you ever experienced living with "divine desperation and holy hunger"? Were you content? Explain.

REMEMBER THIS

When godly passion is birthed in the church, God's presence enters through the door once again. (p. 177)

More Erroneous Assumptions, Presumptions, and Misaligned Paradigms

The process of pursuit begins with "repentance on bended knee," not with religious procedures or proud proclamations of revival. First you enter the "zip code" of God's presence, the realm of repentance and the contrite or humble heart . . .

Once repentance prepares you, it is passion that propels you in the chase to catch Him. (p. 177)

Don't yield to the misaligned paradigm that says there is a formula, a prescription, or a quick fix for every problem in life. God has a protocol or prescribed way of access that is ancient and unchanging. The unholy can approach the Holy only through a Mediator. We have more than a mere human mediator; we have access to God through the blood of the Lamb, Jesus Christ. Even after we receive Jesus as Lord and Savior, we must make repentance a close friend of the heart if we wish to draw near to Him.

1. Compare God's probable response to a proud heart with His response to a broken and humble heart, and describe it.

2. Can you explain how passion propelled you into the chase to catch God?

TAKE IT
PERSONALLY!

It takes a determined God Chaser to deliver what God desires and become a God Catcher. (p. 178)

NOTES

. . . .

. . . .

. . . .

. . . .

. . . .

. . . .

. . . .

. . . .

. . . .

NOTES

12

ONLY GOD CHASERS CAN BECOME GOD CATCHERS

WOULD YOU CLIMB A TREE OF DESTINY TO MEET ME?

God Chasers become God Catchers when they begin to measure time in terms of absences from His manifest presence. (p. 180)

One of the common maxims of financial investment we often hear is, "It takes money to make money." God Chasing has very little to do with money, but it has everything to do with treasure.

We receive our salvation purely by faith in Jesus Christ through the grace of God, yet He commands us to follow Him from the moment of salvation. The Christian life is an investment and exchange of treasure: the more you invest in God, the more He will deposit of Himself in you. It shouldn't be any surprise to learn that only God Chasers can become God Catchers. God plants the tree of divine opportunity, but it is up to you to climb it.

What Do You Think?

Children don't measure the passage of time the way we do. For a little baby, thirty seconds away from Mommy can seem like eternity. The older we get, the easier it becomes for us to handle separation from our parents—and from God's presence. It just gets harder to recover the "joy of encounter" with Him. (p. 181)

1. What do you think? Describe ways that you have grown separate from God.

2. It may be harder to recover the joy of encounter, but how committed are you to try?

Erroneous Assumptions, Presumptions, and Misaligned Paradigms

God is attracted to the "pitiful" side of your personality and life . . . He is repelled by you at your best, but He is attracted to you in your brokenness.

When problems and pain come your way, turn them into altars. Worship Him over your obstacles, and transform your brokenness into a song of desperation to accelerate the chase for the heart of God. (p. 183)

Many people entered the kingdom of God through Jesus Christ, yet they believe that they should always put up their best front for God—as if He is unable or unwilling to peer beyond the borders of Sunday church gatherings and midweek worship services.

1. Perhaps you have already experienced the power released when you turned your pain into an altar of praise and adoration to God. Describe it.

2. Have you noticed that desperation accelerates your chase for God? Explain.

TAKE IT PERSONALLY!

Where do you go when there is nowhere else to go? You hang your toes over the edges of God's promises and "stand still, and see." You may have to worship at "midnight" while you embrace your pain, but the fragrance of your brokenness will draw Him close. (pp. 183–84)

What Do You Think?

Every time you gather to worship Him with other believers, remind yourself, "Maybe this is the night. Maybe He will come again and stay this time."

. . . Your job is to become the fuel of God. Fire without fuel is a smoldering failure waiting to happen, a brief and bright disappointment on the horizon of human hope.

Approach His presence with a burning desire for ignition. (pp. 184–85)

1. What do you think? What role does godly *anticipation of visitation* play in your life and worship before Him?

2. Are you really prepared to become the *fuel of God*? Will you pay the price to approach His presence each time *with a burning desire for ignition*?

REMEMBER THIS

Holy frustration is a characteristic of godly hunger and thirst for God. Be thankful that you are hungry—hunger is the process that keeps your spirit and body alive. (p. 185)

More Erroneous Assumptions, Presumptions, and Misaligned Paradigms

I'm tired of the church being a spiritual thermometer that simply reflects the ambient temperature of society. A thermostat isn't made to merely reflect or measure ambient temperature. It is made to predict and control its surroundings . . .

I pray that someone starts "adjusting the thermostat" in cities around the world. May these desperate "firebrands" turn the dial of passion as high as it will go, saying, "I don't care. I'm not going to stop until the whole city is on fire!" That happens only when someone has had a "suddenly," a God-encounter in the temple or an upper room. It happens when people have "waited" on Him long enough to catch their "hair on fire" and have their tongues touched by the fire of God. (pp. 185–86)

Have you noticed that the church, in general, seems to have a "shut up and blend in" policy rather than a "go ye into all the world" policy? Just how differently do churchgoing people act from those who aren't churchgoers?

1. Are you willing to stand up and "adjust the spiritual thermostat" in your city? What will you do if it brings more "heat" on you?

2. What will it take to ignite the fires of revival in your area?

FILLING THE VOID

I've learned that if you want to _____ His presence, _____ is His favorite _____ and _____ are His favorite _____. When something happens in the _____ of _____ that _____ your heart or _____ your soul, pull the _____ __ you and _____ it to the Lord. There have been times when I felt that I couldn't _____ anymore and _____, but suddenly I _____ ____ there. (p. 186)

What Do You Think?

God doesn't come to you simply because problems come along; He comes because you are *tender*. If you can learn to stay at that tender stage of broken-ness *without* the necessity of contrary circumstances, then you will be "falling *on* the Rock" as opposed to having "the Rock fall on *you*." Both create the same fragrance of brokenness, but one is self-induced and the other one is circum-stantially induced. (p. 187)

1. What do you think? Have you experienced what it is like to "fall on the Rock" and to have the Rock "fall on you"? Explain.

2. Which one do you prefer? What will you do about it?

The people who seem the hungriest are the same people who know how to *worship Him* in spirit and in truth. They have learned to hunger and thirst for the same One they worship and adore. (p. 187)

More Erroneous Assumptions, Presumptions, and Misaligned Paradigms

Will you be a Mary, a passionate box-breaker bearing the fragrance of broken-ness? First, you must abandon the crowd of voices trying to steal or withhold worship from God in the name of preserving man's program . . .

The Father is bending over the ramparts of heaven. He hears the irresistible crackle and the tinkle of breaking alabaster boxes. Is that the sound of your heart breaking? An incredible fragrance is filling the atmosphere, and I hear the rumors of His sudden approach. (pp. 188–89)

The church is composed of people—everyday mistake-making, spiritually challenged Christians who do their best (which is usually their worst). As a result, a local church sometimes finds itself on the wrong side of a disagreement with God (it happened frequently to Israel and Judah). What do you do about it?

1. When I say "abandon the crowd," do you think I'm advocating that you leave the church and chase God as a loner? (Let me answer that: No, absolutely not.) What do you think I *am* saying?

2. Are the "irresistible crackle and the tinkle of breaking alabaster" resonating from your life? Do you think God will hear the sound, even over the din of man's programs or the noisy motions of man going through his religious paces? Are you willing to pay the price necessary to lovingly and humbly pray His presence into your church and fellowship?

What Do You Think?

Mary sacrificed her future for His present presence. What would you give to be saturated in His presence for just thirty seconds? . . .

If it doesn't cost you anything, then it's someone else's brokenness. Worship that costs you nothing is momentary, but worship that costs you goes with you. (p. 190)

1. What do you think? What price would you pay for a thirty-second encounter with the King of eternity?

2. Have you been riding on the coattails of someone else's brokenness? Are you willing to lay yourself and your future on the altar of brokenness so that His presence can bless others?

TAKE IT
PERSONALLY!

Remember, a baby's cry of weakness can access the strength of the Father faster than the speed of light. If you *never* chase Him, you can *never* catch Him. Besides, your weakness will qualify you for a miracle if you put your hunger and desperation on open display. Put a voice to your frustration and cry out to Him. (p. 190)

FILLING THE VOID

Throw off the _____ of man's _____ and religious _____. Follow the path of blind _____. Stand up and let the _____ of a life spent begging for the _____ and _____ of ____ fall away forever. (p. 191)

REMEMBER THIS

Earthly brokenness creates heavenly openness . . . It's as if I can hear the creaking of the heavenly windows beginning to open. It's time to release the cry God can't deny:

"Daddy, I want *You!*" (p. 191)

NOTES

· ·

· ·

· ·

· ·

· ·

· ·

· ·

· ·

· ·

· ·

NOTES

Notes

Chapter 1

1. Tommy Tenney, *The God Catchers* (Nashville, TN: Thomas Nelson Publishers, 2000), 2.

2. Tommy Tenney, *The God Chasers* (Shippensburg, PA: Destiny Image Publishers, 1998).

3. The "answer" to this question doesn't appear in this chapter, but I asked just in case you had some thoughts on it. As I understand the Scriptures, God does not live in time. He created time, just as He created the earth and everything in it. Time "exists" only for created beings who understand what it means to die and who must deal with the side effects of a fallen world, such as physical fatigue, aging, disease, and hunger. Jesus Christ, on the other hand, is the same yesterday, today, and forever (Heb. 13:8).

4. The Scriptures make it clear that God does know your name, and He is very

interested in each of us. (See Pss. 22:9–10; 71:6; 139:13–17; Isa. 49:1; Matt. 18:12–14.)

5. 2 Chronicles 7:14.

Chapter 2

1. Isaiah 6:1.

Chapter 3

1. Luke 9:23.

2. See 1 Corinthians 14:40.

3. God said in Revelation 3:16, "So then, because you are *lukewarm,* and neither cold nor hot, I will vomit you out of My mouth" (emphasis added). Second, the apostle Paul sternly warned the church at Thessalonica, "Do not put out the Spirit's fire" (1 Thess. 5:19 NIV). The New King James Version says, "Do not quench the Spirit." God's intent in these messages is clear and unmistakable.

4. See what happens when a nation of people turns from sin to seek Him (2 Chron. 7:14)?

Chapter 4

1. 1 Corinthians 1:29.

2. From the endnote for this passage, on page 198 of *The God Catchers*: "The Lord pointedly ate with sinners and outcasts (such as tax collectors, non-Jews, repentant prostitutes, and lepers) to the exasperation of the religiously bigoted Pharisees. See Matthew 9:10–13; 11:19; and Luke 15:1–10."

Chapter 9

1. Song of Songs 2:14 KJV.

GODChasers.network

GodChasers.network is the ministry of Tommy and Jeannie Tenney. Their heart's desire is to see the presence and power of God fall—not just in churches, but on cities and communities all over the world.

How to contact us:

By Mail:

GodChasers.network
P.O. Box 3355
Pineville, Louisiana 71361
USA

By Phone:

Voice:	318.44CHASE (318.442.4273)
Fax:	318.442.6884
Orders:	888.433.3355

By Internet:

E-mail:	GodChaser@GodChasers.net
Website:	www.GodChasers.net

Join Today

When you join the **GodChasers.network** we'll send you a free teaching tape!

If you share in our vision and want to stay current on how the Lord is using GodChasers.network, please add your name to our mailing list. We'd like to keep you updated on what the Spirit is saying through Tommy. We'll also send schedule updates and make you aware of new resources as they become available.

Sign up by calling or writing to:

Tommy Tenney
GodChasers.network
P.O. Box 3355
Pineville, Louisiana 71361-3355
USA

318-44CHASE (318.442.4273)
or sign up online at http://www.GodChasers.net/lists/

We regret that we are only able to send regular postal mailings to US residents at this time. If you live outside the US you can still add your postal address to our mailing list—you will automatically begin to receive our mailings as soon as they are available in your area.

E-mail Announcement List

If you'd like to receive information from us via e-mail, just provide an e-mail address when you contact us and let us know that you want to be included on the e-mail announcement list!

AUDIOTAPE ALBUMS BY

Tommy Tenney

NEW!
WHAT'S THE FIGHT ABOUT?

(audiotape album) $20 plus $4.50 S&H

Tape 1 — Preserving the Family: God special gift to the world is the family! If we dont preserve the family, the church is one generation from extinction. Gods desire is to heal the wounds of the family from the inside out.

Tape 2 — Unity in the body: An examination of the levels of unity that must be respected and achieved before "Father let them be one" becomes an answered prayer!

Tape 3 — "IF you're throwing dirt, you're just loosing ground!" In "Whats the fight about?" Tommy invades our backyards to help us discover our differences are not so different after all!

FANNING THE FLAMES

(audiotape album) $20 plus $4.50 S&H

Tape 1 — The Application of the Blood and the Ark of the Covenant: Most of the churches in America today dwell in an outer-court experience. Jesus made atonement with His own blood, once for all, and the veil in the temple was rent from top to bottom.

Tape 2 — A Tale of Two Cities—Nazareth & Nineveh: What city is more likely to experience revival: Nazareth or Nineveh? You might be surprised....

Tape 3 — The "I" Factor: Examine the difference between *ikabod* and *kabod* ("glory"). The arm of flesh cannot achieve what needs to be done. God doesn't need us; we need Him.

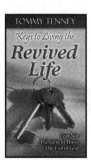

KEYS TO LIVING THE REVIVED LIFE

(audiotape album) $20 plus $4.50 S&H

Tape 1 — Fear Not: To have no fear is to have faith, and that perfect love casts out fear, so we establish the trust of a child in our loving Father.

Tape 2 — Hanging in There: Have you ever been tempted to give up, quit, and throw in the towel? This message is a word of encouragement for you.

Tape 3 — Fire of God: Fire purges the sewer of our souls and destroys the hidden things that would cause disease. Learn the way out of a repetitive cycle of seasonal times of failure.

VIDEOTAPE ALBUMS BY

Tommy Tenney

LET'S BUILD A BONFIRE VOL. 1: "LET IT FALL!"

Video $20.00 plus $4.50 S&H

One hour of the best worship and word from the God Chaser gatherings.

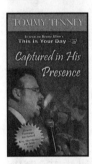

CAPTURED IN HIS PRESENCE

Video $25.00 plus $4.50 S&H

An encounter with God captured on tape! (As seen on This is your day with Benny Hinn)

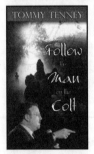

FOLLOW THE MAN ON THE COLT

Video $20.00 plus $4.50 S&H

Are you too proud to ride with Him? Humility is the catalyst that will move your answers from a crawl to a walk to a run to a ride!

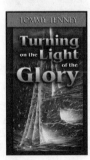

TURNING ON THE LIGHT OF THE GLORY

(video) $20 plus $4.50 S&H

Tommy deals with turning on the light of the glory and presence of God, and he walks us through the necessary process and ingredients to potentially unleash what His Body has always dreamed of.

Run With Us!

Become a GodChasers.network Monthly Revival Partner

Two men, a farmer and his friend, were looking out over the farmer's fields one afternoon. It was a beautiful sight—it was nearly harvest time, and the wheat was swaying gently in the wind. Inspired by this idyllic scene, the friend said, "Look at God's provision!" The farmer replied, "You should have seen it when God had it by Himself!"

This humorous story illustrates a serious truth. Every good and perfect gift comes from Him: but we are supposed to be more than just passive recipients of His grace and blessings. We must never forget that only God can cause a plant to grow—but it is equally important to remember that *we are called to do our part in the sowing, watering, and harvesting.*

When you sow seed into this ministry, you help us reach people and places you could never imagine. The faithful support of individuals like you allows us to send resources, free of charge, to many who would otherwise be unable to obtain them. Your gifts help us carry the Gospel all over the world—including countries that have been closed to evangelism. Would you prayerfully consider partnering with us? As a small token of our gratitude, our Revival Partners who send a monthly gift of $20 or more receive a teaching tape every month. This ministry could not survive without the faithful support of partners like you!

Stand with me now—so we can run together later!

In Pursuit,

Tommy Tenney

Tommy Tenney
& The GodChasers.network Staff

Become a Monthly Revival Partner by calling or writing to:

Tommy Tenney/GodChasers.network
P.O. Box 3355
Pineville, Louisiana 71361-3355
318.44CHASE (318.442.4273)